It's Hell on the Coast

Coast

*A true story of expatriate life in Nigeria,
West Africa, during the Civil War of the 1960's*

Chris Meier

Writers Club Press
San Jose New York Lincoln Shanghai

It's Hell on the Coast

Published by Writers Club Press
an imprint of iUniverse.com, Inc.

For information address:
iUniverse.com, Inc.
620 North 48th Street
Suite 201
Lincoln, NE 68504-3467
www.iuniverse.com

ISBN: 0-595-09903-3

Printed in the United States of America

ACKNOWLEDGMENTS

Thanks to my old friend, Sandra George, for the story of her experiences selling aircraft to the Biafrans.

Thanks to my new friend, Dianne Durawa, for her information on the Peace Corps evacuation.

Thanks to all the Old Coaster friends who still keep in touch, especially John and Lukina Sheldon, Pauline Fiebelkorn, and Carole & Ian Wilson. I hope this will root out more of you! FYI-my email address is cempwm@aol.com.

In Memoriam. *Bill Fiebelkorn, George and Inez Hooper. I loved knowing you.*

CHAPTER 1

There's something about Africa. It has for some people an indefinable attraction which transcends all of the inconveniences and deprivations encountered while living there. It also manifests itself instantly to its willing victims. I first felt it in September of 1966, as soon as I got off the rattly old Fokker Friendship which for the last hour had cast its small, mosquito-shaped shadow over the scrub land and circular native huts of the Northern Nigerian plateau. Seen from the plane, the compounds looked neat and swept, each huddle of huts encircled by a close-grown hedge of prickly pear cactus. Hardly darkest Africa, I surmised, since the passing of the white man's wonder overhead was causing not the least stir amongst the few people who could be seen from that height. Never mind, it was Africa for all that.

I was 23, an English bank clerk married to another English bank clerk. We had both been born and raised in Cornwall, in England's west-country, and had been living for the past year and a half almost 200 miles to the north in the city of Bristol. Tired of being cold, overtaxed, and rained on, we had answered an advertisement in the *Bank Officer* magazine enticingly headed *Your Place in the Sun*. My husband, Tom, had arrived in Nigeria some two months earlier and had written reams extolling its expatriate lifestyle. We were residents of Jos, a small town on the plateau of Nigeria's

Northern State. There was no job offer for wives, but since he was now making more than we had earned together in England, we didn't see a problem there. I was planning on a life of lounging by a pool with a book.

The F-27 contrived to land without anything important falling off. The airport was a Nissen hut equipped with a couple of overhead fans and a very large, very black man whose features were not discernably African. I would later learn that the wide lips and flat noses I had expected to see were the physical attributes of more southern tribes. Here on the plateau most of the people belonged to the northern Hausa tribe. The official wore a khaki uniform and a look of importance. He determined that this particular know-nothing female had forgotten to fill out PUBD forms in Kano, my first point of arrival on the African continent. *Personal Unaccompanied Baggage Declaration*-obviously a most important proce-dure. I understood that the result would most likely be never to see my other two large suitcases again. I wisely decided not to worry about it at that moment. This way without intending to, I fit right into the African nature of things. Wait until you find someone who knows someone and give him a little something to fix your problem. And tomorrow will do.

Outside Jos' tiny airport, the surroundings were beautiful; not beauti-ful in a manicured Palm Beach manner, but beautiful in a wild, untouched-by-human-hand kind of way.

As I looked around, a few drops of rain began to fall. I could smell the rain. Imagine, a place where even the rain is warm! England, goodbye for ever! A single un-edged road led off into the middle distance through a landscape of scrub and rocky escarpments. Scarlet poinsettias as big as dinner plates adorned shoulder-high shrubs on the outside of the airport building. Here and there a figure clothed in flowing robes walked along the edge of the roadway. A woman with a burgundy and gold batik wrapped from waist to ankles passed by, a small brown baby dozing on her back in a sling of material wound around her upper body. A large, deco-rated enamel bowl was perfectly balanced on her head.

Different. Exotic. Not at all like England! This was Africa. The *real* thing! I loved it already.

Expatriates living on the west coast of Africa in those countries from Senegal to Nigeria, which included at that time the Gambia, Sierra Leone, Liberia, Ivory Coast, Ghana, Togo and Dahomey, referred to it as *The Coast,* and to themselves as *Coasters.* Africa's west coast used to be known as *The White Man's Grave.* This slander originated before man's ability to immunize against the many frequently fatal diseases which tended to turn up in places with tropical climates. *The White Man's Grave* attitude still existed in U.K. at the end of the colonial days of the late '60's.

"Better take a machine gun to ward off the mosquitoes...the military...the mau-mau (*wrong country!*) etc." I had actually been the recipient of these fatuous statements. The people making them lived the same kind of lackluster life in England which had already bored me stiff. Wherever the old British spirit of adventure had gone, it was hiding far beyond the vaunted stiff upper lip. This attitude had its advantages, however. A hardship allowance for many postings on the Coast was still in force. This meant that most of the bank clerks, accountants and other expatriate Coasters got an amount equal to roughly 100% of base salary for the hardships inherent in living in nine months of continual sunshine with stewards (house boys) who worked from dawn till dark catering to their every whim, plus gardeners and drivers. The bars and clubs were open virtually 24 hours. There was tennis, golf, swimming, sailing, dancing and every other warm weather leisure activity; and there was three and a half months' paid leave every eighteen months. Aha! *there's* the hardship! Every so often they made us leave and go back to slush, black ice and housework.

The driver who had met me in the bank car drew up at a four-story block of flats. It was a modern-looking building with a rough-hewn stone frontage, set in the middle of a compound where grapefruit, orange, mango and paw-paw trees grew on the front side, and a line of one-story stewards' quarters bordered the rear.

As the driver began to unload my bags, a tall, black man with an unlined round face and neat, upturned nose hurried to the car. He wore a small embroidered cap and a khaki uniform. No shoes. Putting his palms together he bowed his head politely and introduced himself as Garuba, (pronounced *Gahr-ba*) my steward. Laden with baggage…he wouldn't even let me carry my own handbag upstairs…he led me to the third floor and into a spacious apartment where the thing which struck me first was the fact of each easy chair having its own side table.

"Why are there so many little tables?" I asked.

"Is for Star beer, madame," he answered. That was my first intimation of the serious attitude of the expats towards their social life. God forbid you waste any drinking time having to reach down to the floor, or leaning over inconveniently to a central table, to pick up your beer. My suspicions were confirmed as he pointed to a button on the wall above a chair. Every chair had one of those, too.

"Is bell, madame. You ring um for Star beer." Doubtless the steward call buttons have been used for other things, but I already understood why my husband had written so enthusiastically about life on the Coast, and had not seemed to miss our local pub, *The Sailor's Arms,* at all.

Garuba showed me the bathroom, the master bedroom and the guest bedroom, and settled me in a chair with a look of confusion when I told him I didn't drink beer. He was obviously having to revamp his preconceived notion of the English, as my own preconceptions had already been revised regarding facial characteristics. He brought me an orange squash, then proceeded to unpack, bustling past me with armloads of wrinkled clothing.

"Make I go iron um, madame," he explained. Oh joy! Not only do they unpack, but they do your ironing! I thought I had died and gone to heaven.

As I said, there's something about Africa.

CHAPTER 2

Nigeria is divided into roughly three regions by its two major rivers, the Niger and the Benue (pronounced *Ben-way*.) The northern region consists of a broad savanna plateau which slopes to meet the Sahara. Because it is high up and far from the sea it has a climate which is less hot and humid than the south. The little town called Jos, situated high on the plateau, has a particularly mild climate. That and its laid-back lifestyle endeared it to almost all of the expatriates lucky enough to be posted there. I soon met some Old Coasters (since we were at that point almost a thousand miles from the sea, the term *Old Coasters* appeared a bit eccentric) who had chosen to stay on the plateau in retirement. They resided in their lovely houses with their efficient stewards, gardeners and night watchmen, and lived the Life of Riley. One couple who could hardly be bothered to leave, even for skiing holidays, had even made a dry ski run on the grassy slopes of a hill behind their house. Jos had everything!

And Jos was my new home.

It was sensory overload-jacaranda, luxuriant bougainvillea; poinsettias in the large economy size. Smiling Hausa people, who would sing out a respectful greeting while you were approaching, still some fifteen feet away.

"*Sanu, sanu,* madame. *Rank-a-diddy,* master!*" Palms together, heads bobbing. Still greeting us after we had passed them. Giggling. "*Ha ha! See um white master and madame walk? Never get car?*"

True, it wasn't very usual for white people to walk. In fact, some other expat would generally turn up and almost insist on giving you a lift if you tried to stretch your legs anywhere else than on the golf course. All my life amongst the hills and high hedges of Cornwall I had hated to walk. Somehow, on the dusty laterite roads of Jos, surrounded by little semi-naked, dark-eyed pickins calling out "*Sanu!*" and with the odd scrawny chicken underfoot, walking became a pleasure, an adventure.

The Plateau Club was situated conveniently about a hundred and fifty yards behind the bank flats where we lived. Actually, we lived contentedly in both these places. As I signed the club chit for a round of orange squashes and the odd Fanta lemonade about a week after my arrival, one of the other bank wives remarked that she couldn't believe how quickly I had settled in. I explained that some idiot stork had obviously dropped me in entirely the wrong continent some twenty-three years previously. It should have made straight for Nigsville, as it was affectionately referred to by all the Old Coasters.

The club consisted of a large room with a bar in one corner, the usual offices and restrooms, a restaurant, a snooker room with three tables, and a swimming pool into which trailed a purple bougainvillea vine which dangled from the overhanging branch of an enormous mango tree.

After a hard day working on my poolside tan, it was nice to sit inside on the ice-cream colored easy chairs and sip a Pimms No. 1, while the bar steward roasted a dish of groundnuts to keep me fed until dinner. It was hell on the Coast.

The days passed in an idyllic haze. Good old Garuba would cross the compound from his quarters at 5:30 a.m. and wash the car. After that he would cut a fresh grapefruit into interesting patterns, remove every vestige of pith and pip, and pile the chopped flesh back inside the shell for madame's breakfast. Every few days for variety I'd have a slice of glorious, deep orange West African paw-paw, sprinkled with fresh squeezed lime juice. There was also the most delicious, slightly tart orange juice. In Florida, where I am approaching retirement, I have learned that the orange color in oranges is brought about by the rising of the sugar. This is a result of cold weather. That explains why those juicy West African oranges were always green and yellow. No cold weather! It made it a little difficult at first for me to choose ripe citrus, but that wasn't a problem. Garuba usually did the shopping anyway.

Not far from Jos, many hundreds of miles from the sea, was Pan Yam fish farm, of all things. My very first meal in my new home had been Garuba's deliciously fried prawns. One day, in a fit of guilt over having nothing to do but enjoy myself, I decided to make prawn cocktails for dinner without benefit of Garuba's input. It wasn't until we began to eat them that I discovered you are supposed to cook them first. So much for fresh seafood. In U.K. the supermarkets had always served prawns ready-cooked and cleaned. As far as I was concerned, that was sufficient proof that God had not intended me to be a cook (especially when He had provided me with one as good as Garuba!)

I was free to spend my mornings at the pool with a book, or on occasion to visit Kingsway. Kingsway department stores were an institution in Nigeria. Virtually every town of any importance had one. The canny managers saw fit to include a coffee bar so that when the expats required a change from the bar at the club, they could all meet at the bar at the store. As there was no fresh milk available in most of the country, coffee in West Africa in those days meant using either Millac milk powder made up into liquid form, or else pouring straight canned evaporated milk into your cup. No problem there, I loved both.

At Kingsway we always checked out the meat department first. Whenever a stock of imported meat hit Kingsway, the first expatriate woman to discover it would hurry to the phone and pass on the word before rushing back to the counter and stocking up. The recipient of the phone call would undertake to tell another madame while grabbing her shopping bag and car keys preparatory to doing her own Kingsway raid. Eventually the word would get around town, the meat locker would empty, and then we'd wait a couple of weeks until the next shipment. Of course, the local beef was almost always available. This was known as Bauchi beef. Bauchi was a small town located miles out in bush to the north of Jos. We went there once, and found insufficient incentive ever to repeat the journey. Mostly I remember that the pool was small and about one-third filled with a thick, green slime. I think it was most likely the home base of some of the more exotic tropical bugs we hear about these days.

The cattle in Bauchi weren't bad really while they were in Bauchi. It was just that they would be walked to their eventual slaughter, which took off the fat and rendered them somewhat chewy. In Jos this wasn't a major problem. However, in Lagos, a thousand miles to the south, Bauchi beef was obviously not looked upon with a great deal of favor. I liked it because you could buy a large hunk for only ten shillings and when stewed into a curry it would feed half an army.

We got almost everything from Kingsway. Our main household effects shipment got sidetracked somewhere for seven and a half months. So, we bought our china and cutlery from Kingsway, likewise what cooking and baking dishes our steward didn't borrow from other stewards in the block of flats. It wasn't unusual for dinner guests to remark on the similarity of the casserole dishes to the ones they had been given as a wedding present. Steward would go on serving chop, acting as innocent as the day is long.

I arrived in early September, 1966. I was soon advised by the other wives to send off Christmas cards by sea mail that same month, since the bulk of them would be going back to U.K. and the postage would be prohibitive if left to go by air nearer Christmas. I only did this the first year as my mother-in-law received hers the following week but my mother's had not yet materialized by Christmas Eve. Kingsway, of course, was the source of my Christmas cards. They were beautiful too...colored pictures of vivid scarlet Flame of the Forest trees in full bloom, frangipani in yellow, pink and white, and bougainvillea in every shade of purple and peach.

My most pervasive memory of Kingsway is set to a Jim Reeves record. Whoever was in charge of the Jos Kingsway record counter, which was conveniently located next to the coffee bar, was *the* Jim Reeves fan of all time. The records *He'll Have to Go, In the Misty Moonlight*, and *Four Walls* must have been played gray, and in my memory still accompany coffee laced with evaporated milk.

Leaving Kingsway was an experience. Ninety percent of the beggars in town would cluster around the car, each trying to open the door for the occupants in the hopes of getting a dash, in this case a few pence.

"Hello, madame! Please, madame! Gimme dash, madame? God bless you, madame!"

Their afflictions were of every kind: blindness, missing or horribly deformed limbs, even inability to walk. Some crawled. From the first I was struck by their attitude. They were always pleasant. Possibly this stems from the assumption that more bees will be caught by honey than vinegar, but they would smile and I didn't see that they had much to smile about. Sometimes an officious store employee would attempt to shoo them away, but I always let them be. I even became fond of one, a young teenage boy on crutches, whose head was bent slightly sideways and whose left shoulder was several inches higher than his right. In spite of his twisted body he had a particularly lovely smile, and he knew I liked him best. So did the others. Soon they would let him be the one to open my car door and receive the shilling dash. There were coins for some of the others too. I still can't subscribe to the theory that if you don't give to beggars nobody will beg. If you don't give to beggars they will go hungry, is the more likely result.

Once I dropped my handbag on the road while fishing for coins for the beggars. There was an immediate chorus of, "Sorry, madame! Sorry! Sorry!"

"It wasn't your fault," I said. That was before I discovered this is a normal expression of sympathy from a West African. I noticed that nobody tried to steal the bag, in spite of the dark warnings about beggars and thieves which had followed me during my last days in U.K.

This universal sympathy cry is always well meant but sometimes not well understood. Our friends in the adjacent flat, Ron and Celia, had a baby a few months later. Its birth was eagerly awaited by all the local bank staff as well as the expatriates. The baby arrived. It was a beautiful little girl. Ron proudly went to work to spread the good news.

"Baby done come!" he yelled across the main banking floor. "It's a girl!"

"Oh sorry, master! Sorry! Sorry!" came a chorus from bank clerks, secretaries and guards alike.

"Whaddya mean, sorry?" said Ron. "I'm *pleased!*" This totally confused the bank staff. *After all, does not every man want a son? Maybe master say he want girl to save face.*

CHAPTER 3

The custom of dash is inherent to Africa. It was not introduced by colonialism and I think that the early colonials did their best to stop it. That didn't work. I believe the general feeling then was *if you can't lick 'em, join 'em.*

A dash is a gift or a bribe. Little or no distinction is made. It can take the form of a small tip for keeping an eye on your parked car *("Make I go lookum your car, madame?")* or simply a gift, like a Christmas gift, for instance. It is a token of gratitude for a favor, too. This sometimes evolved into the feeling that the token should come first to ensure the successful completion of the favor. The attitude has been stretched to include even the performance of one's job, for which a paycheck would in any case be forthcoming from another source. The custom of dashing was rare in a job-related capacity during the colonial days when the British set up the governmental rules and offices. As control was handed over, however, more petty officials began seizing the opportunity for augmenting their personal incomes. My steward told me that his brother (all fellow tribesmen are *brothers*) had been required by the passport issuing clerk to dash thirty pounds plus a bottle of imported brandy in order to obtain a passport. I was more disturbed than Garuba, who shrugged and accepted this fact of life…particularly in view of the fact that it was the going rate. Thirty pounds represented almost four months' salary for a steward, and the cost of the brandy was half as much again.

We usually resorted to a dash as a means of settling small problems, but it didn't always work. There was the afternoon I decided to play snooker with young friend Liz. The steward wouldn't unlock the club snooker room, explaining that only persons over eighteen could enter.

"But I'm 23! I'm a madame!" I exclaimed, pointing futilely at my wedding ring. He smiled politely and continued to believe that I was a troublesome teenager out for the summer holiday. I even offered him a shilling, but he smiled and refused. That was a first! We got it sorted out later with the help of the lady manager, but that was my first inkling that Africans frequently have the same trouble categorizing us as we do them. When I had lived there for a while I got fairly good at guessing a person's tribe, though I never did very well with guessing ages. Maybe he was just a new steward.

Snooker, the European version of pool, played on a bigger table with slightly more curved pocket-edges, was a major pastime on the coast. We had some excellent players. The usual game was called *Volunteer*. After sinking the first red and taking the free ball which followed it, the player could "volunteer" any color he wished. If he did not pocket a volunteered ball, then he gave away the number of points for that color, or four points, whichever was greater. No color could be volunteered more than three times in succession. It did teach you positional play in order to make the most of three consecutive colors. The scores reached the 300's and there would be some fancy stuff involving three consecutive blacks, pinks and blues, and the snooker room would frequently get as noisy as the rugby field. We were frequently late home to dinner because of the activities in the snooker room.

One of our snooker partners was a very polite, pleasant and rather quiet young man named John Major. He arrived on the coast a few months after I did and his official title was that of Assistant Accountant, the same as my husband. He had moved into a flat on the floor above us, sharing it with another young man who could best be described as an engaging young reprobate. Not so John, who never undertook anything he couldn't write home about, even at the age of 23. While many of his peers were whooping it up (or worse) at Madame Fulani's, (the local *House of Joy*) he would engage in an evening's snooker with us. Chatting while awaiting our turns, he once mentioned that he considered West Africa a temporary posting. His intention was to return to U.K. and go into politics.

"Politics!" I echoed with scorn. I couldn't imagine why anyone in their right mind would want to leave Africa in the first place, but politics....!

"Why on earth would you want to do that?" I asked, and did my best to dissuade him for the rest of the evening. So, had he listened to me, Britain would in later years have had to make do without one of her most fair-minded and honorable Prime Ministers.

At the club there was also cinema on Thursday nights. The club stewards would place chairs in neat rows under a roof which stopped some fifteen feet short of a whitewashed wall, like the screen from an American drive-in. We would select a chair and move it. Sometimes we would select two or three and recline across them. Depending on how bad the film was, or how out of sequence the reels were shown, we might end up chatting in groups just as though we were still inside the main club. The stewards would be bustling to and fro with drinks, and the only people actually watching the screen would be the throng of locals peering through the wire fence along the edge of the club property. Garuba was always among these. He was an inveterate moviegoer.

We had dances at the club almost every Saturday too. I enjoyed these hugely. Everyone turned up from way out in bush, and with a ratio of nineteen white males to one white female, you would have had to look like a frog not to be in demand. There appeared to be some kind of unwritten rule requiring three dances with each partner. This didn't change anywhere on the Coast, and dancing provided most of us with our main exercise. Sometimes there was no opportunity to sit down all evening.

The dance music at the Plateau Club was the product of a large pile of 45 rpm records, many slightly out of date. One was *Blue Tango*. I always loved the tune, but I never learned how to tango. Neither did most of the other women. A local Middle Eastern bank manager loved to tango. He would lunge back and forth through the other dancers, crushing his partner to him and using their outstretched arms as a battering ram. Whenever the DJ steward put on *Blue Tango*, most of the women present would suddenly take an urgent trip to the powder room until the record was over. It used to get pretty crowded in there.

In Jos, where places to spend money were very limited, it was common practice to send a bottle of champagne to the table of any lady who took your fancy. The men would build a pyramid of wide-mouthed champagne glasses and pour the bubbly into the top glass. It would run over and fill the glass below it and so on until all glasses were filled. That bit was fun. It was the taste of the stuff which I never did learn to enjoy, but this presented no problem since there was rarely a chance to sit down and drink, anyway.

Fielding the usual, "What's a girl like you doing in a place like this?" type of question and sporting a new cocktail dress every Saturday, any female could get to feeling like something special in the wilds of darkest Africa. A call from a bunch of friends at our table would interrupt whatever dance I was doing at the time, "Hey Chris! Another bottle of champagne! From matey at the bar!" Smile nicely, and later raise a glass in that direction. It was hell on the Coast.

The best West African institution is the curry lunch. A West African curry consists of white rice, a large pan of curried beef, chicken or shrimp, and about forty side dishes. The curry is made with coconut milk and since the beef and the chicken tend to be tough the sauce is stewed a long time until the meat is ready to shred. The side dishes include fresh and fried pineapple, banana, tomato, onion, coconut and peppers. Nigeria has wonderful peppers, almost all of which are hot enough to knock your socks off. There is very often *stinkfish*: powdered, dried fish which is very well named. I think this is also known as *Bombay duck*. Groundnuts (peanuts) are employed both fresh and roasted, and a delicious sludge made of fried garlic, okra and tomato is often included. Add whatever fruits and vegetables are also available and you have your basic West African curry.

It is customary to welcome new Coasters by giving a curry lunch in their honor. So it was that the day following my arrival, which happened to be a Sunday, we had driven the nine miles to Bukuru (pronounced *Buk-aroo*) for my first curry chop. Bukuru was a small township which is chiefly known for having the highest incidence of lightning in the world, which they say is due to the amount of tin just underground. It's true that on any evening, entertainment could be had on our balcony simply watching the flickering in the skies over Bukuru. In fact, there was an occasion, while we were talking on the phone to a friend in his bank office, that a mighty crack ended the conversation. The phones were out for a while, not an unusual condition. When they were reconnected, our friend told us that a lightning bolt had struck his receiver and hurled him off his chair. Luckily, he was unhurt.

This Sunday was the day I learned that it might be billed as a curry lunch, but don't expect food to be served before mid-afternoon, following prodigious amounts of Star beer quaffing. I even went to one curry lunch which was served as late as 5:30 p.m. Many of the guests I had met the previous evening at the club's Saturday dance. There were about 25 guests altogether, mostly bank personnel. Apart from the great food, I remember the occasion for the amount of laughter and bonhomie. We had the sort of good time that characterized most expatriate get-togethers on and off the Coast. Everyone had a tale to tell of some hilarious misadventure, usually in communication. Celia, who lived across the hall from us, had just received three Marks and Spencer's cotton bras from England. The customs official had requested 100% duty on three musical instruments.

Thinking to settle the problem, Celia had unwrapped the package and displayed the contents. No luck! The customs man had decided on musical instruments, and duty on musical instruments was what he intended to collect. This was greeted by shouts of *WAWA! (West Africa Wins Again!)*

Everyone had something to add. It was great fodder for my weekly letters home. The talk turned to famous Old Coasters, and so to an eccentric expatriate bank inspector, who was named John Wright. I did see this person once in later months when he entered our company flats by climbing up the ornamental stone on the outside of the building and vaulting over the balcony. Your average white man used to use the stairs. (No lifts of course, not with *that* electricity!) This man was a legend in Northern Nigeria, and his fame had spread as far as Lagos, a thousand miles away. As an itinerant bank inspector, his job was to go from bank to bank, through bush, jungle and desert, ensuring the accuracy of the records and the moral rectitude of those chosen to serve in the profession of banking in general, and his employer in particular. He was a slim man dressed in a khaki bush suit, mostly remarkable for the tight fit of the little shorts. He wore a knife in the back of his belt.

John Wright's territory encompassed towns like Kano, located in the Sahara, so he would usually ride a camel. Camels had less mechanical problems than cars and were easier to fuel in bush. There were many tales of John and his fully integrated life-style, complete with silverware and sundowners in the bush, but the best concerned his racing camel. He had one of those too. There is a great difference between your common or garden everyday camel and a genuine racing camel, (mainly registered in mph,) and it was his racing camel he rode one day to the Kano Club. He tethered it outside in the car park alongside the patrons' cars. During its master's sojourn in the club, the camel died; and during its death throes it trampled a neighboring MG, totally writing it off! *WAWA!*

At this, my first curry lunch, I heard for the first time the most famous chop (food) time story of all-the one about the suckling pig. Some Very Important Persons were coming to dinner and one madame had designated suckling pig as the main course. Instructing her steward on the finer points of serving it, she admonished, "A suckling pig should be held aloft on its way to the table, and it is always served with an apple in the mouth." (Kudos to her for getting an apple in the first place! They don't grow in Nigeria's tropical climate and need to be imported. They are rare and costly.) At the high point of the banquet, the suckling pig was borne triumphantly into the room by the steward, who held a large red apple clamped firmly between his teeth, just as madame had instructed! *WAWA!*

Another *WAWA* story in the same vein concerned a couple who moved to a new house which had a serving hatch. At their housewarming dinner party, madame told her steward to be sure and remember to serve chop through the serving hatch. Her back was towards the kitchen and it took the look on the faces of her guests to make her turn around…in time to see the steward completing his climb through the famous serving hatch, platter balanced on high.

Someone else countered with the fact that their steward had served celery and custard for dessert just last week, and the talk grew more personal. Our host also came in for some good-natured teasing about a coffee-colored pickin strongly resembling him at Madame Fulani's, the local House of Joy.

It was a great lunch, and only lasted until 11 p.m.! Bert Kaempfert's *Swingin' Safari* LP was very popular at that time. We played it continually through-out the afternoon and evening. The wealth of anecdotes was punctuated by the high yodel of *Wimoweh,* and the record still invokes fond memories of my first curry lunch.

CHAPTER 4

Insulated as we were in our pleasant little world on the plateau, with week old newspapers arriving on Sundays from London and reception on the radio less than desirable due to the constant fluctuations of ECN, (*Electricity Company of Nigeria,*) we usually did not find out what was going on in the big, bad world until it had gone.

A scant few weeks before my arrival, a coup d'etat had disposed of the military leader, Ironsi. The expats don't waste too much time worrying about these things since as long as the Star beer factory keeps up production there is obviously nothing to worry about. Besides, one new friend swore that there was a new coup every Thursday and the worst inconvenience about that was trying to remember the name of whoever was in power that week. A few rumbles and rumors reached the plateau regarding some reprisals for the last coup, which were taking place in Kano, the largest city in the north, situated on the fringes of the Sahara desert. The problem was probably some of the usual inter-tribal warfare, since Nigeria housed some 250 tribes, each with its own language or tribal dialect, and several religions. The north, populated mostly by Hausa and Fulani, was strongly Moslem. The west was controlled by the Yorubas, (pronounced *YOR-uhba*), a political people who were predominantly Christian, although the God of Iron was worshipped in some areas of the mid-west around Benin, and, I believe, a bunch of other minor gods as well. The forested eastern regions were mainly Ibo, more educated due to their longer interaction with sea travelers and resultant longer-standing opportunities to *savvy book* (read.) The Ibos were also mostly Christian. There was plenty of voodoo about too. In West Africa, where it began, it goes by the name of *juju*.

Regardless of what the white man in Africa hears, the natives hear it first because their communications system is superior. Telephones have nothing on tribal drums. I heard that at some point the colonialists outlawed the drums. They make the expats nervous. They certainly do make the hair stand up at the back of the neck. The real reason for outlawing the drums had to be the way their speed of communication left the white man at a disadvantage. Lying in bed at this time under a great, romantic tent of mosquito netting, I could hear the muted thunder of the talking drums through the open windows, far into the night. My blood would race in response.

What took place in Kano we later found out to be a massacre in Sabon-Gari, the Foreigners' Quarter, which was populated mostly by eastern tribes. Resentments or reprisals, whichever they were, culminated in the northern tribes attacking the populace of Sabon-Gari with machetes, old hunting rifles, broken bottles…. anything that came to hand. Within a few days the problem spread to the northern cities of Kaduna, Gombe, Sokoto (pronounced *SOK-a-too*), and Jos.

On the morning of what we were wont to refer to as *The Troubles*, I had decided to go over to the club pool and work on my tan after breakfast. Before I had finished my prettily carved grapefruit, Garuba shuffled up, head bent, and muttered something which sounded like, "Madame not go for town today."

Totally unaccustomed to Garuba suggesting what I should do with my time, I asked, "Why ever not?"

"Is better, madame," he mumbled, not looking me in the face.

"Why not?" I repeated. He wouldn't elaborate. He just looked shame-faced and backed into the kitchen. I suppose in retrospect he wasn't supposed to say anything.

At 23 I was not accustomed to going anywhere without full makeup, down to two coats of mascara. Sitting at my dressing table fiddling with a bunch of cosmetics, I could see out of the window where a mob of Nigerians was half running by, brandishing every home-grown weapon from broom handles to machetes. This wasn't anyone's regular behavior. I also noticed that without exception they wore their Nigerian dress, loose, flowing *agbadas* or long, Arab *djellabas*. It was very unusual to see no western dress. Clerks in particular liked to affect long-sleeved white shirts, ties and western style trousers, and to grow long the fingernail on the little finger of their right hand for turning pages. This showed everyone that they could *savvy book*.

The mob ran around the flats and headed for the club. I called for Garuba, but he was nowhere in evidence. As he was a good Moslem who observed the five prayer rituals every day from his ring of stones in the compound, this was not unusual. Moslem stewards all took a few moments for prayer several times a day, and since they only asked for a half day off on Friday to attend the mosque, and not the whole of Sunday like the Christian stewards, nobody objected to the prayer breaks.

There was a thumping at my door, and a woman's voice yelling. Since Garuba didn't answer it, I did, mascara brush in hand. My neighbor Valerie from one of the downstairs flats was outside. She said with rising panic, "Come across the hall to Celia's. There's some sort of riot going on. We should all stick together."

"O.K.," I said equably. "Just let me finish the other eye."

"No! *Now!*" She almost screamed. Which was how I came to be sitting next door with a bunch of frightened females, balancing a small mirror on my knee.

"How can you think about makeup at a time like this?" someone demanded nervously.

"I might as well finish the job. I'd hate to have to be evacuated or chopped with only one eye made up!" Not a very good attempt at lightening the situation, but to tell the truth I was mildly miffed at anything getting between me and my tan. It was becoming obvious there would be no pool time today. When you have spent 23 years in England looking for sunshine you tend to be greedy about it when you get it.

Looking through the trees at the club didn't tell us much. Once or twice a running figure could be seen. Sometimes more than one. The mob came back down the road and returned towards town. Our men came home from work.

"We've had to close the bank early. All the eastern staff have gone for bush. We are afraid they might get chopped."

Out of the 35 bank staff, about 30 were Ibos or other eastern tribes. This was a fairly usual percentage. It had become a point of resentment among other tribes that the easterners always had the best jobs; but then, as I have explained, the northern herdsman had had much less opportunity for education and were in any case often reluctant to work outside of the strictures of Islam.

Bits and pieces of the situation came to light as other expats arrived at the flats seeking shelter. Many were too nervous to stay in their houses and needed the security of being surrounded by their own kind. Also, many Ibo stewards were missing and the heck with being alone *and* having to cook your own meals!

The first thing done in Africa following any sort of political upheaval is the imposition of a curfew. I didn't realize that this would be the first of many during my stay on the Coast. It didn't seriously inconvenience us. Although we missed the club we had the company, as the flats were filled to bursting with temporarily displaced friends. There were enough stewards between us to round up large, pot-luck dinners, and the building resounded to noisy card games of *Chase the Ace* well into the night.

Our hilarity was dampened greatly by some of the news items, however. Robert, one of the club stewards, had had his hands cut off. It was rumored that he had run for bush after that. We prayed he got away. Friend Ian, who managed a branch bank down in the Nigerian section of town, risked his neck sheltering his steward of many years. Mark was an Ibo and had to be transported to the police station compound where easterners were being rounded up preparatory to flying them down to the coastal areas. They would be safe there where their tribesmen were in the majority. Six-foot Ian drove a little MG sports car. Stuffing Mark down the back and covering him with an old mat, Ian drove the length of the main drag, Ahmadu Bello Street, to the police station. By the time he returned, all of us at the flats were sick with fear for him. His poor wife, Carole, held up very well during that ordeal.

The refugees at the police station were apparently in a terrible state. Many had broken bones, wounds caused by machetes, and organs which could be seen protruding through unbelievable slashes. Nurses were needed at once. Of all the wives at the bank flats, two had been registered nurses back in the U.K., so Jo and Valerie went bravely into the fray. Their husbands drove them to and from the police station, again receiving no impediment from the mobs, who were still wandering the streets brandishing home-made weapons. We were agog to hear the stories on their return.

"You aren't going to believe what we did!" They told us. "*We* don't believe what we did!"

They had spent the whole evening stitching the wounds of people who should have been dead. Some victims had had their skulls split with machetes. Val and Jo had been stuffing brains back in and stitching the flesh back together. They were shell-shocked. They explained that the skull bones were noticeably thicker in many of the wounded than any they had ever seen, and that fact had undoubtedly enabled the victims to live through blows which would have killed any white man. They had stitched, splinted and bandaged for hours. They were definitely the heroines of the day.

Other victims who came to our attention included a poor fellow in the compound of an Old Coaster named Doug, who lived on the far side of town. Crossing his yard one morning, Doug passed a tribesman engaged in ramming the end of a broom handle into the rectum of a yelling victim. Pausing in his work, the attacker greeted Doug with traditional respect, "*Rank-a-diddy*, master!"

We agreed with Doug-the policy of non-interference in tribal matters was sometimes hard to follow.

In successive weeks we heard of this person or that person who got chopped, and this or that steward of many years' standing who went for bush, stopping only to take with him a bonus of bed linen or extra stores. Everyone was philosophical about that. We understood that when you flee for your life you probably need to take the closest provisions at hand.

Of all the bank wives, only I had been a bank clerk in my old life. How long ago that seemed, back in boring old England! In spite of that, all wives were pressed into service for a period of about three weeks while new local staff were hired and trained. Business must go on. So, for a while I forsook the pool and went back to work. I enjoyed my stint at the bank in its prestigious location at the end of town, and the interaction with the colorful personnel who worked there. I particularly remember Audu (pronounced *Ow-do*) Kano, the proud warrior who was No. 1 Bank Guard, and whose impressive uniform was completed with crossed swords. Real ones. His sidekick was nicknamed *Syphilitic Adamu* (pronounced *Adam-oo*) by everyone in town, and even he had probably forgotten his real name. He was a small man, far gone in the ravages of venereal disease, with eyes almost blinded, rotting teeth, and a general demeanor which looked as though he were on his last legs. I thought it was kind of the bank not to let him go.

Some of the staff were colorful characters too. One, whom we nicknamed *Big Thick Gabriel* with references to the size of his body and his lacking IQ, took a shine to me and proudly presented me with a book, *The Satan Bug*, because he had noticed that I liked to read paperbacks. He mentioned with a hopeful smile that a transistor radio would make a nice return gift.

I enjoyed working the Burroughs 200 statement machines under the tutelage of the beauteous Elizabeth, a quiet female bank clerk from a local tribe who remained from before the troubles, and I also acted as my husband's secretary. Then wives got discharged from emergency banking and were banished back to the pool, the club, Kingsway, and the Lebanese dry goods stores along Ahmadu Bello Street. So things returned to normal. The curfew was lifted. New clerks and stewards were hired. Western dress was seen once more in the offices and on the streets. Bikinis were seen at the pool.

An estimated 30,000 people had died in *The Troubles*. One more massacre, in a series whose beginning dates from the beginning of African history, was over. They still continue today.

In a reprisal for this reprisal, some 400 northerners returning by train, due to ill-feeling in the south, were set upon and butchered by Ibo soldiers. A few weeks later we were talking with a friend who had been staying in Lagos when anti-northern feeling there burst forth in another localized massacre. Pregnant women's bellies were slit, and legs severed as the victims tried to run. Northerners were lying dead in pools of blood all over the road, prompting an eastern (Christian) acquaintance of our friend to make a joke out of it with reference to the Hausas' Moslem religion. On Islamic holidays it is customary to slaughter sheep to be eaten after sundown.

"Look!" he laughed. "Dey look same t'ing sheep at Ramadan!"

CHAPTER 5

Tom and I were very alarmed when Garuba announced his intention of returning to Biu province to enter the family business. (Especially me. Housework is definitely against my religion.) I tried everything I could think of to dissuade him. He was as usual quiet, polite, and adamant.

In those days a steward on the plateau was paid about eight pounds a month, plus a dash of about a pound for extra work entailed each time there were dinner guests. He received three free uniforms, two khaki for regular days and one white for special occasions; and any discarded clothing from the employer's family was usually given to the family of the steward. It could be worn or sold. As in the far east, it was a matter of face not to overpay a steward compared to the going rate, and as in the far east the stewards usually took it upon themselves to make some minor compensations. By far the most common of these was to appropriate a few staples from the larder, particularly sugar. It was quite usual to hear one of the madames say, "Oh, my steward is completely honest. He only takes about three pounds of sugar a week."

We usually just bought extra. It was a good bargain at that.

So it was that I couldn't offer Garuba the earth to remain, but I did my best to make it worth while for him to stay. As it was, he promised to find me another good steward.

"Mind you teach him to make curry as well as you do!" I cautioned.

The day came when he brought for my inspection a boy who looked about fifteen. He looked northern, perhaps mostly Fulani. He had fine bones and great, slanted doe eyes. Garuba introduced him as Abubakar (pronounced *A-boo-b'kar*.)

"You be small boy?" I asked with suspicion. A *small boy* is a kind of apprentice steward, usually a helper in a large family. I could see I had hurt his feelings and immediately felt guilty.

"No, madame. I be steward." Eyes downcast.

"Oh, I'm sorry. You look so young. How old are you?"

He said he was 21 and I felt that he must be lying to get the job. It turned out that he was married and his wife gave birth to their first child some months later. I agreed to give him a trial as a steward. If he, and particularly his curry, passed muster, he would remain.

"We'll call you *Garuba II*," I said, not expecting him to be around more than a week, so there didn't appear to be any point in learning to yell out a new name.

I was so wrong! Garuba II turned out to be one of the all-time great stewards. He liked to think of things to do to please me. One day he emerged from the kitchen proudly holding aloft a magnificent cake. It was freshly made, and he had cut it twice and inserted layers of whipped cream and sliced fruit. He was obviously anxious for me to try it. Since I had been out to lunch I had no room to eat, but being careful of his feelings since our first meeting, I had the bright idea of calling the other expats from the block of flats and having an instant cake and lemonade (and Star beer) get-together. It was a great success.

Soon after he began working for me, I thought I heard him say, "Yes, darling" in answer to some question. Feeling that I must have been mistaken, I shrugged it off. Later a visiting friend asked incredulously, "Did he just call you *darling*?"

"1 thought I heard him say that yesterday," I said. "Maybe he hears my husband say it and thinks it's the proper way to address me. I am not going to make a big deal of it, though. I have already hurt his feelings once and it's not fair to rub it in if he's that inexperienced. He's turning out to be a great steward."

Eventually my husband heard it and explained that as a title, *Madame* would do. As it was out of my hearing we hoped that Garuba II felt face had been saved.

There's no doubt his steward's zeal was undiminished. Every meal was an adventure. The chicken would be stuffed with butter, for instance. His Chicken Kiev was excellent. On the same plate the onion would be stuffed with spinach and the tomato with peas. Although you rarely got the right innards with any particular food, everything was delicious.

Your average steward didn't have it easy. The houses and apartments of the expats were at the least more than adequate, and at the best, gorgeous. This did not necessarily extend to the kitchen, however, since there was no reason for anyone to enter it except for the household staff. Therefore the steward worked his wonders without a ceiling fan or air conditioning, and sometimes with less than adequate utensils, since many times shipments of household effects would go astray for months, as did ours.

I wandered into the kitchen one afternoon to check on a half-Siamese, half tabby kitten named Snowy, which my husband had recently brought home. Snowy was evincing more than a passing interest in a cupboard from which I could hear a muffled squawking.

"What's that noise?" I asked.

"Dat de dinner, madame," Garuba II replied.

I flung open the cupboard door to find an indignant chicken squatting on the shelf; a typical Nigerian specimen, scrawny and paranoid. Until then it had never occurred to me that chicken for dinner for us meant that the steward had had to buy, catch, kill and clean the bird before he ever started cooking. It did teach me to be less critical of some of those chewy fowls.

CHAPTER 6

Other organizations besides the banks were hit hard by loss of their staff and so jobs opened up in many locations throughout the north. I went to work as secretary and bookkeeper to a Syrian importer who owned a chain of hardware and fancy goods stores. His previous secretary had been a white girl married to an easterner who lived in Jos. They had had five small children. It had apparently not been a union made in heaven. In order to make sure that the kids were fed, she tried to keep her paycheck each month. According to Mr. Kahale, my new boss, her husband would hit her in the head and face with her shoes until he got the money from her. My new boss told me worriedly that he was sure she was dead, and that her husband had probably taken advantage of the general exodus of eastern tribes and gone for bush, or back to his tribal homeland.

My new boss was a wily old man who still had all his ducks in a row at age 72, and who used to write all his cost prices in Arabic so that the authorities wouldn't know the extent of his profit. This meant that the first thing I needed to do was learn to write Arabic numbers. It followed naturally that I'd learn a few words, and I came to appreciate spoken Arabic as a very sensible language. A few root words turn up constantly and other words are obvious derivations. Sometimes it makes for entertaining mental exercise linking nouns and verbs. For instance, the verb *to write* and the word for *ring* are a lot alike. You can work out for yourself that in the early days of writing, much of the signing was done with a seal ring. The words for *cold* and *refrigerator* have a very obvious connection. I like words and discovered an interest in Arabic. After pidgin English, Arabic was the most widely spoken language throughout the African continent, spread by Islam and also by the ubiquitous Lebanese and Syrian traders.

I had our Lebanese and Syrian friends to thank for another major discovery in the realm of diet, after the famous curry chop. Middle Eastern cuisine is very popular in Nigeria and the European expats were almost all great fans of *hummus, m'tabel, kafta* and the glorious garlic-laden Lebanese barbequed chicken. One of the most memorable meals during my sojourn on the plateau was given in my honor by my Syrian boss. It included the most delicious chicken I have ever eaten, stuffed with rice, almonds and pine nuts.

He spoiled me in many ways other than via the goodies from his kitchen. The office overlooked one of the few rose gardens in Nigeria, and he would place roses and fresh picked pomegranates on my desk. Incentives to learn *worrdi* (rose) and *roman* (pomegranate)! His number one Mercedes sedan was mine during working hours to run his errands, and when my old Opel Kapitan languished for a month awaiting a new alternator, it was my boss who handed over the keys to an old Volkswagen on indefinite loan.

His beautiful, sloe-eyed daughter, named Samira, also lived in the house behind the rose garden. She was only a year or two older than me, and found various excuses to visit the office. Her father encouraged it as a way to illustrate his disapproval of my suntan.

"Why you do this to yourself, ya Chris?" he would ask. "Our women prize their beautiful light skin and they do not go out in the sun."

There's no explaining a sun addiction like mine to someone who comes from a place where they get lovely weather most of the time! However, his plans went a little awry when, not only was I unmoved from my goal of looking like my steward, but Samira became restless with tales of *actually being able to go swimming whenever one wanted to go.* Such unbelievable happiness, it seemed to her.

"I went swimming once when I was little," she said. "It was wonderful. Sometimes I dream about it."

Good Moslem women don't flaunt their arms and hair and bodies in public, and swimming from a public beach for a full-grown woman was unthinkable. I felt sorry for her mainly because they become full-grown women at such a young age, which leaves so little of their carefree childhood to enjoy. A neighbor along the same street was quite the most beautiful woman I had ever seen, and when I asked Samira if she and Nadimi were friends I was told, "Oh, not really, she's only a child!" The girl was 13. I would have guessed 19 at the least; (and move over, Miss World!)

My dear boss tried hard to civilize me in other ways. Hearing curses resulting from broken nails at the typewriter, he sent away to Germany for the best Pfeilring manicure set available and presented it to me as a Christmas gift. That sapphire nail file was in use twenty-five years later; although I still don't pay adequate attention to my nails.

Life was idyllic. Garuba II cooked. The sun shone. There was plenty of company at the club. On many weekends a group of expats would foray into bush or along the dusty laterite roads to the Yelwa Club at Bukuru, or even farther to Barakin Ladi. Laterite is either red dust or red mud, depending upon whether it is the dry season or the rainy season. If it was the dry season and you kept the windows open, then you arrived a light pink shade with a heavy thirst. If it happened to be the rainy season and you arrived, that was a plus in itself. One weekend a couple of Old Coasters were bent on showing my husband and I the suspension bridge at Miango. I envisaged a bunch of plaited lianas slung across a gorge. I shall never know, since half way out in bush our four-wheel drive vehicle became so hopelessly bogged down in the center of the laterite road that it cost all of our small change dashing everyone we could hail to help push us out. We had to turn back.

There were two all-day excursions from Jos into the bush which are still fond memories. There was the time when about a dozen of us decided to go to see the duck-billed women of Zaranda. The location was about 60 miles out in bush and was found by watching the speedometer until an exact number of miles had passed, then making an abrupt left turn past a large mango tree. Zaranda itself was unreachable by car, but on certain days the women came to another village to the market, and we would see them there. Sure enough, a contingent of natives, naked but for a small bunch of grasses slung low from the hips, milled amongst the regular inhabitants of one of those neat little circular hut villages that I had seen from the air on my initial flight across the plateau. In accordance with the centuries-old tribal tradition of beauty, the women had had holes made in their ear lobes and upper and lower lips. These holes were filled with flat, circular plugs of calabash. Larger plugs would replace one another until the ear lobes hung to the shoulders and the lips poked forth three or four inches, making eating an art. Another most individual feature was the hair, cut to little more than an inch all over in length and caked into a hard helmet with what looked like the famous red laterite mud. The effect was slightly reminiscent of a wartime German soldier at the western front.

Entrepreneurism takes all forms. In an area where the opportunities for making money are severely limited, it had quickly been learned that foreigners were willing to pay money for taking photographs of anything. So our change changed hands and the local lovelies posed with their babies, and with us, and with each other. When we arrived at the market, the main articles on sale appeared to be local cigarettes, sold singly for a copper or two, filled with who knows what, and hand rolled to a degree of neatness I had never seen in Europe. These cigarettes turned out to be an acceptable substitute for coins, and some locals preferred them.

Ian, who had lived several years on the plateau, had warned us not to part with the last of our pennies as we should need them to get away. The only way to clear the populace from the cars was to scatter the remaining pennies from the car windows and take advantage of the resultant rugby scrum to drive off. Not too many outsiders took that trip through the bush to the market village, and I suppose you couldn't really blame the inhabitants for not wanting to see the departure of the few sources of revenue to turn up each dry season.

En route home from that excursion, we visited one of the loveliest spots I have seen on the planet. One of the passengers remembered the way, and directed us down rutted tracks, under great guava trees laden with over-sized strawberry-shaped fruit, and around the monstrous boulders which strewed most of the plateau area. Walking the last few yards, we burst out of the grass onto a small river. It was fed by a small waterfall which fell some 25 feet, splashing onto the big, gray rocks by our feet. At the top of the falls, two hibiscus bushes peered over the edge with their shocking pink blossoms bright against the blue sky. It was fun to splash around in the calf-high water. Since the *bilharzia* fluke is endemic to many parts of Africa, all bodies of water which are not swift flowing are eschewed by the expatriate population. This particular parasite can enter through the skin and takes up residence in the liver, whence it weakens the body and can eventually cause death. I never met anyone who had had it, but because of its existence, we always played in swimming pools, large rivers, or the ocean, and ignored lakes and ponds.

We left, reluctantly, when we had all run out of film. Unfortunately, our pictures didn't develop and at that time it was not possible to get color prints in many parts of Nigeria. Never mind, it would have taken a better photographer than I to capture the impact of the pink hibiscus with the blue sky and the white, frothy water. The memory will never fade.

The other never-to-be-forgotten excursion involved about 25 expats who decided to take a picnic and go climb the Shere (pronounced *Sherry*) Hills. In my defense, I must say that it didn't look that hard a climb from the bottom. It is said that several countries could be seen from the small radio station at the top. Most of the women, who had more sense than I, decided to stay at the foot of the hill with the picnic stuff and the drink.

I was wearing shorts and a sleeveless silky top, and on my feet were a pair of Bata's flip flops made of some yellow man-made pseudo-rubber material. *Bata* was the name of a chain store selling most of the footwear to be found throughout Nigeria. Sir Edmund Hillary probably never recommended this particular climbing outfit; but as I said, things didn't look that difficult from where I stood. I soon discovered that those flip flops had a tendency to turn my foot over painfully every few steps.

It seemed like a good idea to follow a dried-up river bed, since the small stones might not offer the best footing but didn't hide snakes or scorpions as well as the elephant grass might. A couple of the children in the party soon turned back, as did a few adults. I was impressed to see childless Ian swing a toddler onto his bare shoulders. The kid made it to the summit that way.

About three hours into the physical misery of this venture I decided that dying would be a good idea, and sank to the ground in a messy heap. Some fellow sufferers persuaded me to keep going since we were almost at the top and there would be water there. Liars. What there was turned out to be one rusty rain barrel with about four inches of soggy sludge in the bottom. In Africa you must boil water, then filter it. Then you put it in the fridge and soon become accustomed to your drinking water coming only from such a source. Frankly, on this occasion I didn't care. I scooped up some faintly liquid sludgy stuff in a discarded tin and rinsed the stuff around my mouth. God alone knows why I didn't catch everything from the Black Death to Housemaid's Knee (not to mention bilharzia, of course.)

I hardly remember the famous view. There was bush, plain, and purplish mountain as far as the eye could see in all directions. So much for that. The only thing of interest to me in the entire world was a drink, and the heck with snakes, scorpions, the possibility of breaking my leg, or anything else between me and it. I took off down the hill by the direct route, deliberately ignoring those meandering stream beds. Mostly the elephant grass and bushes were about the same height as me, but you don't have to see clearly to know when you are on a steep down slope. The going is considerably easier than the other way. I made it down in less than twenty minutes and aimed straight at the picnic wagon. I didn't even have the decency to answer questions about the whereabouts of the others until I had poured down half a gallon of lemonade (somebody gently removed that before there was none left for the other survivors), an entire Star beer (I hate beer! I have always hated beer! and I didn't care!), and moved on to the liquid which came with the jungle juice. In Nigeria, *jungle juice* refers to a delicious fresh fruit salad of pineapple, banana, pawpaw and oranges. This one had been liberally spiked with kirsch by the picnic organizer. I didn't care about that, either.

Never had I been so thirsty. Never have I been in so much pain, either, as during the days following this particular exercise. Every muscle from the ribs down ached. For a week I had to descend the apartment stairs slowly and backwards, to the consternation of the Migardi, who already doubted my sanity from the occasions that I left my husband sleeping his Star off in the carport, instead of heaving him up three flights of stairs.

Mine weren't the only injuries. All the idiots who had climbed the hills were creaking and cursing for days, and the combination of sun and wet-diaper friction across Ian's shoulders from his small passenger made for some obviously very painful peeling.

I did learn a lesson from my experience. Future exercise on the plateau was restricted to dancing at the club and lifting soup plates of curry chop.

CHAPTER 7

I have said before that I think Arabic is a sensible language. Spoken, that is. I still don't write it. Hausa is also sensible from my point of view. The night watchman, for instance, is a *Migardi*. My guard, see? In Jos there was a quaint little zoo. Its attendant was referred to on the signs as the *Zukeipa*. That makes sense; as did the road sign admonishing the motorist to slow down for a dangerous *Korna*. Of course I am assuming these words are Hausa but I guess it is perfectly possible they are more forms of pidgin, which has long been a source of surprise and delight to the expat on the Coast.

Pidgin English includes a smattering of French derivative, which is understandable in view of the fact that much of the West Coast was originally colonized by the French. The most pervasive word of all, *palaver*, has its roots in the French verb *parler*, meaning *to talk*. Perhaps due to the fact that in many tribes much of the talk tends to degenerate into high-spirited argument, the word *palaver* tends to mean trouble more than just regular conversation. *Hell of palaver* could be used to describe a punch-up at the club as much as an inter-tribal skirmish.

When my husband had first arrived on the plateau, his first encounter with pidgin involved the barber, who arrived at the home of a friend during lunch-time.

"Wait small, barber," said David.

"Why are you calling him a small barber?" asked my husband, eyeing the six foot visitor with due puzzlement. It turns out that *small* can mean *a little while* or *a little bit*, and a very tiny bit will be referred to as *small small*. Works for me!

Daily speech quickly came to include "Pass chop" for "Serve the food;" and soon "Pass water" didn't even occasion a raised eyebrow. It is interesting to note that *to chop* means both *to eat* and *to kill*, which again made sense. References to a person being chopped, however, tended to remind one of Nigeria's colorful past. It was rumored that some tribes out in bush still liked long pig, but we ignored this as being Old Coasters' tall tales. The word *bush* meant anywhere that there weren't many people; but calling a Nigerian a *bush man* was a deadly insult, the very opposite of being able to *savvy book*, for instance.

The wash, done almost daily by the steward with the aid of any handy sink, drain or river, is a source of rich communications snarl-ups. It's confusing enough that the English and American languages have so many discrepancies; for instance an item of feminine under-wear referred to as *knickers* in English becomes *panties* in American. Stewards tried to keep to either English or American households the way we kept to certain tribes for stewards. It minimized foul-ups. For the most part the Coast was European-oriented, and the Nigerians would refer to all expatriates as *Europeans*, which used to infuriate the Americans. From my English viewpoint I thought it highly amusing the way that one pair of men's underwear became a *pant*, although I have since found it quite common in America. There was the time, though, that I came totally unglued when looking for a bra which did not return with the wash. With the aid of considerable explanation and pantomime I tried to get through to

Garuba. Finally the light dawned. "Aha," he said, "Madame mean *knicker-for-up.*"

After many years of living on the Coast, some white men develop a remarkable facility for jabbering away in pidgin with great fluency. Visiting some friends on one occasion I learned how to ask for Austrian smoked cheese, which comes in a cylindrical shape.

"Steward," said John, "Make you go bringum dis cheese him same t'ing sausage!" Obvious, really.

All visitors to the Coast sooner or later come into contact with the pidgin version of the Book of Genesis. This hilarious translation of the first book of the Bible gives things a genuine African slant. Noah's Ark is immortalized as Elder Dempster, (the only steamship passenger line plying the West Coast on the Africa-Europe run,) Gabriel blows a trumpet, *"de Lawd he say 'Aha,'"* and Adam's reaction to Eve is, *"Eh Lawd, she be fine pas' stinkfish!"*

Another source of amusement is given names. Why any race which gives its offspring names like Zak, Edith or Oscar can afford to laugh at any other race beats me, but we did get a kick, as it were, out of Longtoe Bonyu. His mother explained that when he was born, his main physical characteristic was that one of his toes was long. So-explain away Zak!

Many children's names were a result of a whole-hearted admiration for the white man's wonders. On the plateau and later in Benin City I met many Bicycles. Perhaps the best, though, came after an expectant Mum had visited a gleaming new bank building on the plateau, which had the boss's title in gold leaf on his door. When Junior arrived, she named him Manager's Office.

The Nigerian tribal system is rich with titles. They do not always translate directly in English to something we can understand, like Earl or Lord. Many derive from a feudal system of sorts, and many carry prodigious responsibilities towards lesser members of the tribe as well as prerogatives of rank. In the north, the Emir of Kano was one of the greatest chiefs. In tribal and religious tradition, he had more than one wife. Being a progressive man he had a palace built in the European tradition. Being practical women, his wives used the bidet as a receptacle in which to pound *gari,* the cassava which represents their staple diet.

Great respect was accorded to chiefs and men of rank, and in Northern Nigeria a Moslem who had made the pilgrimage to Mecca and had thus become an *Alhaji* was, as our English friend Ron put it, "The bloody same as Jesus walking around on earth." An ordinary Moslem mister translated as *mallam,* a fact which couldn't be passed up by the local expat theatrical group, which put on the hysterically funny skit, *Call Me Mallam.* Other musical offerings included *Salah* lit. *Prayer Days,* after the word for the Moslem feasts, and *The Idle Fitter,* after *Eid-el-Fitr',* one of the most important of the annual Moslem holidays. We really appreciated those holidays. Being fortunate enough to work in a country encompassing several religions meant that we got all the feast days of all the religions as holidays. Christian holidays come on the same days each year, but the Moslem calendar goes by the moon and thus the dates can alter from year to year. During one February holiday at the pool, I remarked to my friend Marie that we had hardly been to work at all in December and January, what with Christmas and Ramadan and everything.

She wriggled back on her lounge chair and ordered another drink. "It's hell on the Coast," she said.

CHAPTER 8

Christmas on the Coast was wonderful. A couple of the bank personnel in the flats had children, and were heard constantly complaining of how deprived their offspring were not to be enjoying Christmas in good old soggy England. I did try to understand. Not hard, though.

In Nigeria, Christmas doesn't begin in August as it does in less civilized environments. We had sent off our Christmas cards in September to minimize postage costs to U.K., and after that we could safely forget the whole thing until about the second week of December.

I knew I was going to enjoy myself the first time I heard *Jingle Bells* played on a Hawaiian guitar over the speakers in Kingsway, while the sun shone brightly on the traders with their wares spread under a flame tree, and I realized the only work that would be required of me on Christmas Day would be to dress myself.

The parents of the UK-Christmas deprived offspring had subtly hinted that it would help the kids get over their disappointment if those of us who were childless each bought some little thing at Kingsway and wrapped it to put under their tree. When I saw the resulting stack of parcels I figured that we didn't have to worry about too much disappointment unless due to the difficulty of finding room for all of the loot in one of those flats.

I was delegated one job, however. It had been decided in a fairly dem-
ocratic way that we would have a Progressive Christmas Dinner. Cocktails
would be in one flat, turkey and trimmings in another, dessert in a third,
and coffee, nuts and burps in a fourth. Celia and I would get the turkey.

I was brought up poor, myself, and hadn't ever had a turkey. I did enter-
tain a mild suspicion though that in good old Nigsville I wasn't going to
find one hanging upside down in Kingsway's meat department. Right. I
also figured that since Celia was very pregnant at the time it might fall to
me to accomplish this turkey task. Not necessarily true. She did her bit.
Also, we used her car, and owing to the state of the boot afterwards that
fact was definitely above and beyond the call of duty.

We drove off into bush in her little Opel Kadet and eventually arrived
at this turkey farm, or whatever it was. The obliging owner took our
money and pointed at a large (to me) and antisocial bird running around
behind the bushes. The farmer could have made a mint out of a video
(had they been invented) of Celia and I skidding around in some type of
Two Stooges routine, missing the darn bird in all directions. It just *knew*
it wasn't going to like it if we caught it. It was right. It occurred to me that
the bird was going to be as scrawny as Bauchi beef if we ran it around for
another hour. We eventually cornered it, braved its gobbling and pecking,
and stuffed it in the boot of Celia's clean little white Kadet. That was our
bit done. When we got home we left it to the Migardi, two stewards and
a gardener to get the homicidal fowl out of the boot (talk about the
Augean stables!) and clean up after it. I hoped we dashed them enough to
make the whole business worthwhile.

The turkey turned out pretty well, really. It was my first and I hadn't had
to slave over a hot stove all morning, so I wasn't disposed to be critical. The
children had gifts for days and they didn't appear disposed to be critical.
The adults had Star beer for days, plus an excellent selection of liqueurs
that some influential Swiss bank customer had dashed the staff as a
Christmas present, and they weren't disposed to be critical. Snowy, my cat,
had the time of her little life batting into oblivion the few tinsel Christmas

tree balls I had been able to get at Kingsway, so she wasn't disposed to be critical. Altogether, I thought it was a most successful Christmas.

I did miss going to the pool, though. Christmas Day celebrations were not the only reason for a lack of pool-lying during December and January. At this time of the year the dust from the Sahara Desert gets stirred up and clogs the atmosphere in all directions, sometimes for a distance of a thousand miles. This weather phenomenon is referred to as a *harmattan;* obviously, we decided, because that is what its chief job is-to harm a tan. The sun's rays just can't get through the haze and there were times when I lay poolside at the Plateau Club and couldn't clearly see the other idiots opposite. The harmattan exacerbates the dryness of the air in areas close to the Sahara. Another result was the splitting of our beautiful local carvings because of the lack of moisture.

West African art is magnificent, and its carvings are particularly impressive. Every expat's house was to some extent home to a collection of heads and figurines, animals and masks. During the harmattan when you heard a loud crack, as from a gun, you learned to go and check your carvings to see which one had suffered this time. Oiling them in advance didn't always work.

The first time I heard the crack of a splitting carved head (*splitting headache,* as my husband later referred to it) I looked over the balcony to see if anyone was shooting at our Migardi. He, for all his fierceness and pride, was armed like most other tribesmen only with a machete, a bow and some arrows.

The only way the harmattan really inconvenienced us was the way it messed up plane schedules. Certain imported items which should have arrived by plane didn't, and if you planned to go on leave you couldn't guarantee that the plane would take off and you might traipse back and forth to the airport for a week before visibility improved enough to catch the F-27 to Kano. As Kano was located in the Sahara it had worse harmattans than we did, and you might get stuck there another week. I never felt it was a problem though. It was getting stuck at the other end that bothered me. That happened once due to ice on Heathrow airport runways. We ended up taking a terrible flight via Belgium on Sabena (*Such A Bloody Experience-Never Again!*) and returned to my beloved Nigsville a day late. I'd much rather *leave* Nigeria a week late!

So, we continued to lie around the pool, and once in a while we'd watch a dust devil scurry across the tennis courts. Once one veered abruptly in our direction and blew Ron's clothes into the pool. Nobody wanted to dive in to retrieve them. The pool got cold during the harmattan season.

On January 1st., 1967, as we lay about in our usual poolside positions, we heard a rhythmic drumming. It was accompanied by a sound like maracas and came from the other side of the pool wall. Clambering on the back of a couple of lounge chairs we could see a line of native dancers approaching the club. Everyone grabbed a wrap and watched some of the best entertainment I experienced during my time on the Coast. We thereafter always referred to them as *The New Year Dancers*. Nigerians of some northern tribe (we never discovered which one), dressed in belts of hanging monkey tails and cloth headdresses, danced at the back of the club for a long time. The maraca-type noise came from the plaited reeds tied around their calves. Seeds had been trapped inside the reeds and rattled with the movement of the dancers' legs. The sound of the drums stirred me to memories of the nights during *The Troubles*. I realized that the sound of African drums is one that always elicits a visceral and emotional response even in an expat. Somehow you feel that they are speaking to you, you just don't fully understand the text.

The day a dreadful blow fell was one of those days when the harmattan had been gone long enough for my tan to have fully recovered. We were making plans for this and that excursion off the plateau before the rains came, and the world was beautiful.

This particular item of unwelcome news arrived home with my husband at the end of the banking day. A transfer! The fact of it being a promotion for Tom in no way compensated for the misery of leaving the plateau. There was also no way to refuse. Being sent back to England would have been worse. We were going to Benin City, capital of Mid-Western Nigeria. I cried for two days. My poor, dear Syrian boss was distraught.

"If only your husband worked for a local company," he kept saying. "I would dash them five hundred pounds to keep you, and that would be the end of it. The trouble with these British is that they won't take a dash."

I agreed with him there. Mind you, I did stop sniffling long enough to be flattered at the amount of the dash. On the plateau, thirty pounds would have practically got you ownership of an entire tribe.

CHAPTER 9

As the plane circled for its landing at Benin City, the view did nothing to assuage my longing for the plateau. Mostly I could see dust. Red laterite dust, of course. There were dusty red roads, dusty red palm trees, and corrugated iron dwellings with roofs red from dust and from rust.

A bank car delivered us to our apartment, which was situated above the bank itself and was accessible via two outside stone staircases. Its location at the meeting point of five laterite roads in the town center made the bank a sort of Nigerian Arc de Triomphe amid a red dust Etoile. The cacaphony of traffic, people and chickens which arose from this maelstrom through the windows opening on all sides of our new abode was daunting. I later blamed it directly for burning out the condensers on my record player, since in order to hear Elvis I had to play his records with the volume full on. Meanwhile, from the little open-fronted stores which lined the roads all around us, speakers would blast the popular local *high life* dance music at a nuclear decibel level. A rattly old air-conditioner was cemented into the wall of the bedroom. We kept this running much of the time in order to drown the outside sound-effects. As far as cooling goes it was particularly underwhelming. Luckily, I have never felt the heat and the lack of air-conditioning was not a problem. Cold is entirely another matter. Benin was a lot warmer and more humid than Jos. I immediately enjoyed the sensation of leaving the bedroom and having the thick warmth of the African night envelop my whole body, and curl around my toes. The heat did a lot to encourage me in settling down to a new life.

Much of our lifestyle was the same as in Jos. There was Kingsway, there were innumerable expat parties, and there was a club.

The Benin Club was not as big or attractive as the Plateau Club, and it was not as much a center of life for many of the expatriates, except on cinema nights or Mondays when everyone would turn up for badminton. Badminton was listed under *Night Games* on the club bulletin board, which sounded interesting enough to lure a couple of dozen white-clad men and women over with their racquets for a couple of hours. Besides, they could drink Star while they played. They swore that attendance had soared since management had changed the wording on the club board to *Night Games* from *Games Night*.

The friendly attitude of expats in any foreign location was as prevalent here as in Jos, and in no time we were completely assimilated into Benin society.

A new friend appeared late one night following an unbelievable crash from the direction of the back door. Leaving the bedroom to investigate, we discovered a bearded young man with a very Scots accent making himself at home in the living room. He introduced himself as the local bank inspector. Another madman? This category of people encompassed more than the usual eccentrics. It probably came from being alone in bush too long. When in town he always stayed at the bank flat and was accustomed to unlocking the back door by giving it a hefty kick with his jungle boot. The resultant crash as it flew back against the wall was what had awakened us. Not only us; the poor little bloodless-looking gecko lizards which lived on the ceiling and chomped away at high-flying mosquitoes were sent into a positive frenzy and were falling off their perches everywhere. Later when I'd forget my key and use the same method of entry I would be just as startled as the geckos when a couple of them fell on my head.

"Didn't our night watch give you a hard time?" I asked.

"Nah, he's always asleep," replied our new guest. I never saw the Jos Migardi take a nap, I thought to myself.

Our Benin nightwatch, however, was a plump and cheerful Buddha who felt not the slightest twinge of conscience at snoring the night away…and he wasn't that easy to wake up. We didn't feel that we had anything worth stealing anyway (that household effects shipment was *still* lost, and didn't in fact turn up for 7 ½ months) so we didn't bother to complain to the bank and have him sacked. We did make it our business to wake him up every so often, though. It turned into something of a game. We would come home from the club or a party at some ungodly hour, and there would be the nightwatch in his sleeping wrapper, rotund and snoring on a bench by the bank wall. We would drive quietly up to a distance of three feet, then turn on full headlights as we blasted the car horn. The nightwatch would come alive in a tangle of weapons and wrapper and would fall off the bench. Then he would swear up and down that he had not been sleeping.

Equally as lacking at being a steward as this useless individual was at being a night watchman was George, bequeathed to us by our predecessors. The previous bank wife was more duty-bound than I and actually oversaw the cooking. She would give very specific instructions to the steward, such as to turn the meat when the timer rings, and peel the potatoes and boil them, etc. etc. My sole housekeeping duties went as far as, "Steward, we have sixteen people coming for chop." I might add, "Let's have curry," but I usually didn't even get that detailed.

Needless to say George didn't last. The catalyst was our guest bank inspector, who liked his breakfast egg boiled exactly three and a half minutes. He gave George precise instructions. When the egg was served it was practically raw. Ian Frazer, the inspector, had been living on the Coast long enough to know how to get to the heart of things.

"George," he said, "Did you cook this egg exactly three and a half minutes?"

"Yes, sah!"

"Do you have a watch, George?"

"No, sah!"

"Then how did you time it, George?"

"I done count, sah."

"How did you count, George?"

"One-two-three-four," etc. (at a fair gallop.)

"And how many did you count?"

"Fifty, sah!"

Even with some tried and true stewards it was as well to poke your head into the kitchen once in a while to check on progress, particularly if there were to be dinner guests. The Bank of America manager was somewhat bent out of shape once when dinner was very late in spite of his steward having a host of friends in the kitchen helping out. A quick inspection proved that they were all engaged in trying to stuff the ground meat mixture into each separate spaghetti noodle. *WAWA!*

John followed George in our kitchen, but not for long. He was much given to grunting blankly. All cooking was done by individual propane gas tanks. John would leave the stove on until the gas ran out, then when we came home from the club for dinner he would not have made any because there was no gas. When we asked why there was no gas (since we had refilled the tank only two days before) he would explain that was because it had run out. When we reiterated he wasn't to leave the flame on unless he was cooking he would grunt blankly.

Adding to the general confusion was the fact that in West Africa it is usual to say *yes* in answer to a negative question, meaning that the assumption made in the question is correct. Since this is foreign to our method of speech, we usually rephrased the question or tried to become more specific. Things just got more confused. On John's last morning I was a little short of patience because of a lack of gas again, and was making a list to do my own shopping at Kingsway. I didn't think John would be up to that.

"John, there's no chocolate milk left in the fridge, is there?" I asked.

"Yes, madame," he answered. I immediately realized I shouldn't have phrased things that way, but made matters worse.

"Yes there is or yes there isn't?"

"No madame." I tried again, this time phrasing it the right way around.

"Is there any chocolate milk in the fridge, John?"

"Uuuugh?" Grunt and blank look.

"Milk, chocolate milk!" More specifics.

"Uh, there is pineapple, madame."

"Pineapple! Jeeesus !"

"Cheese! Yes, there is cheese, madame!"

My husband left for work, muttering darkly that the bloke who shook the first tree had got a lot to answer for.

After several other trials and tribulations, we found Mamadu. Actually, he found us. This skinny individual, older by a good thirty years than Garuba II, turned up at the door one day offering well-thumbed references and a wide and cheerful smile. He was wonderful, and changed our entire lives. He was the Binni equivalent of Garuba II and he looked after me like an old mother hen.

I remember my 24th. birthday. I had had the total lack of organization not only to be born on the wrong continent, but in the middle of the rainy season. The rain was pouring down so I couldn't lie around the pool or play tennis, and there was no diversion to be found at Kingsway or any of the little native shops along Forestry Road. I was bored, and since this was a very unusual state of affairs I was prompted to lie on the floor listening to Elvis records and reflecting on the end of my useful life.

Mamadu took pity on me. He bustled in with a dish of freshly roasted groundnuts and a cup of coffee with lots of evaporated milk, just the way I liked it.

"Oh Mamadu," I wailed. "Do you realize I'm 24 years old today? I'm getting old and useless!"

"Ah, madame!" he laughed, throwing up his hands like an old biddy. "You be still small pickin!"

I should have thought to ask him his age, although our stewards frequently didn't know exactly and would usually just say what they thought we'd like to hear. (I'm still not convinced that Garuba II was twenty-one.)

Mamadu was a character. He was dependable, efficient and an excellent cook. He wouldn't move into the bank compound because he had a family and a house across town. Whenever I gave him cast-off clothing for his family I would see him later wearing it himself. He had no worries about losing his machismo and we'd see him negotiating the bank steps in my old gold and white flip-flops, wearing a decorative button-through cardigan and holding aloft my lemon yellow pagoda umbrella. The expat bank staff enjoyed the sight and tried to persuade me to donate cast-off bikinis in the hope that Mamadu might use them to brighten up his morning coffee run to the downstairs offices. It was all in fun. His perpetual grin was as popular with the other staff as with us. We had no end of offers to employ him when the time came for us to go home to U.K. on leave.

Mamadu also had a feel for what might amuse madame, and one evening he pointed out with a grin our rotund nightwatch scuttling around the compound with a large jar after a feisty land crab.

"He goin' chop um," explained my trusty sidekick.

"Shall we help?" I asked.

"Sure t'ing, madame!" he replied, and the two of us raced down the steps and around the compound, scaring the daylights out of several wandering land crabs and ensuring a tasty supper for the family of the nightwatch. Several of his friends came over to join the fun. Sometimes coming home in the car, the headlights would wash over a large number of crabs. Then various natives bent on catching dinner would risk life and limb running in front of the car to get at their prey.

In Jos, another nighttime feast had been provided by sausage flies, but none turned up while we were in Benin. This was just as well, seeing it was too hot to keep the windows closed in that tropical, aircondition-less environment. A sausage fly is a revolting looking insect of about an inch or an inch and a half long. Its body looks just like a fat, brown sausage. The flies swarm at certain times and don't look very carefully where they are going. They fly straight into closed windows with little banging noises, and if the window happens to be open they fly through it, across the room and straight into the opposite wall. When they fall to the floor they walk dizzily around in circles, buzzing constantly. The natives think they are delicious and collect them in jam jars. I used to yell at the steward to come and get any which ended up indoors. He was welcome to them.

CHAPTER 10

Luckily for me, the pool at the Benin Club was completed less than three weeks after my arrival. Before that, the closest swimming facility was the pool at NIFOR (the Nigerian Institute For Oil-Palm Research.) This attractive acreage was far enough from Benin that most people did not make the trip unless for a full day at the weekend. The facility had more than 1,000 varieties of palm tree, and a clubhouse with a pool which was drained, scrubbed and refilled every couple of weeks. It was not always the beautiful, clear blue which we have come to expect of swimming pools today. However, weekends there were fun because most of the Benin expats would be lying around sunning, playing with their children, and generally having the indolent good time we had all come to expect from life on the Coast.

Palm oil was used in cooking, apart from other things. On one occasion I mistook the palm oil chop served at NIFOR to visiting expats for my favorite lunch, since it was served with rice and side dishes, and I suffered the results of eating large, oily mouthfuls of meat in a reddish sauce that I could have sworn looked like curry. Another painful eating experience which I can only blame on myself involved some small, yellowish apples I found growing on a tree near the pool. These were cashew fruit. Sticking out from one end was a thick, hard casing, slightly half-moon shaped. Before my neighbors could yell a warning, I tried to bite through the hard casing to get at the nut. Mother Nature fills the casing with acid, which works pretty well in keeping predators away from the ripening fruit. Except for me, that is. I had burns around the sides of my mouth which kept me out of trouble for a long time.

I was never bored if I could fry myself in the sun for anything up to eight hours a day. It was at this point I sickened myself of science fiction. Some previous occupant of the bank flat must have been the greatest sci-fi fan of all time since there were 92 science fiction paperbacks in the book-case and very little else. I read every one consecutively. I have never read a science fiction novel since!

Fewer people were around to use the new Benin Club pool than in Jos, and I made friends with a cocky little Lebanese named Saidi, who owned three cinemas in the area. I soon had him improving my Arabic as a change from reading sci-fi, and would lie in the sun pointing at lizards and giggling "*harrdoon*". I always had this priceless vision of a lizard in a tam o'shanter and kilt, since the Arabic word *harrdoon* sounds so Scottish to me. For sure it will the last Arabic word I'll ever forget.

Lizards are all over Nigeria, and they were my main source of amusement at the Benin club pool. Divided into three stripes of gray and orange and sometimes as long as seven or eight inches, they would skitter beneath the lounge chairs and run up walls in search of bugs. The canny lizards would spot prey high on the face of a wall and run up the wall on the opposite side of the corner, out of sight of the victim. Then with a sudden dart around the corner the lizard would chomp down on a struggling dinner that never had a chance. I used to wonder how the lizard knew exactly where to run around the corner. After all, the distances involved had to be up to twenty times the length of the lizard itself. You'd expect the creature to miss by a couple of feet once in a while. The *harradeen* (Arabic plural!) appeared particularly fond of some huge and lovely moths with about a six-inch wingspan and shocking pink target marks on each wing. When a lizard zeroed in on one of these moths and caught the hapless insect in its jaws, the result resembled a biological airplane with a gray and orange fuselage and brown and pink wings.

The reason I returned to work wasn't so much that lizard-watching palled as conversation indicated a desperate need of some secretarial organization in Saidi's cinema business. When he determined that he was being ripped off by one of his cinema managers we decided I would fix his system of cinema receipts and catch the offender. I went to work for a couple of hours every other day and had a good time, although suffering a shock at his filing system. When Saidi received a letter he would throw it in a cupboard. If he ever needed to refer to it he would open the cupboard door and sit on the floor amid the stuff which fell out, and see if he could find the letter. I mentioned that if this was the way he had been handling his box office receipts then it was amazing he was still in business at all. Things improved when I had made up some files, written some letters, and inaugurated a ledger or two.

The main cash shortages indicated that the problem was in Warri, a town about forty miles away to the south. We took a trip there one day in Saidi's large new car. Luckily it was not yet the rainy season, though we had gone hardly ten miles when the windscreen shattered. It was probably stress caused by the world-class potholes in the road. My miniskirt wasn't much protection and my thighs were scratched and bleeding a little, but this was no real problem. We had stopped to brush the shards of glass off the seats when Saidi yelled at me to get back in the car quickly. A black, moving mass approached from a jungle trail a few yards away. It was a column of ants on the march, maybe two feet wide. We couldn't see where the column ended but Saidi gave me to understand that I didn't want to be in on the beginning of the column, either. From where we were parked we could see that the vegetation beneath the creatures was entirely eaten away, and Saidi wanted out before they started in on his precious new automobile. I was a little disappointed as I would have liked to take a closer look. Still, it was exciting. For all that this was darkest Africa I hadn't seen anything wilder than some ten foot high termite hills up on the plateau.

I had been warned to take some perfume with me for use on the ferry at the Sapele (pronounced *SAP-uh-lee*) River. Nothing prepared me for the stench from the lorries filled with raw rubber which made the river crossing on every ferry. The jungle area in the mid-west is prime lumber country. There is even a wood named after the town of Sapele (although wrongly pronounced.) Rubber plantations abound. In West Africa, when rubber is tapped it runs into calabash bowls and congeals. The resultant raw rubber comes away from the bowl in the shape of a thick, smelly bathing cap. It is a smell of elemental Africa and I am told you can get used to it; however, it proved too much for me and cost me half a bottle of *Arpege* on a man's handkerchief to get across the river. That was the only African smell which I couldn't learn to like or tolerate. Later on, the storm drains of Lagos never bothered me. I connected them in my mind closely with Africa, which I always loved, and anything which has reminded me since of that smell still overcomes me with waves of longing.

We stopped for lunch at the Sapele Club. I liked it a lot. It was more attractive that the Benin Club and the food was good. Mostly I noticed the pack of small, green-haired expat children. The steward who took care of the pool was obviously enthusiastic about the use of chlorine. Natural blondes turn a pretty shade of pale green if they spend a lot of time in an over-chlorinated swimming pool. All expat children in Nigeria learn to swim by about two years of age, and it is difficult to use the diving board due to the hordes of little kids jumping off with screams of delight and swimming back to repeat the process. I have seen kids do this for four hours at a stretch. Pool fun was obviously the main activity of these children.

The interview with the rotund cinema manager in Warri resulted in a collection of contradictory, if inventive, explanations for the cash shortages. Saidi sacked him, then spent much of the journey home bemoaning the fact of having to find and train another manager.

He did have his problems. I found many of them hilarious. The whole social thing of the cinema in West Africa was hilarious. The main cinema in Benin was the Atlantic Cinema, and Wednesday was Expat Night. This meant that the film would be in English and hopefully not more than a couple of years old. We'd sit in the air-conditioned balcony and attempt to see something, anything, over the headdresses of the Nigerian ladies in the first couple of rows. When she goes out dressed up, a Nigerian lady will invariably wear a head-tie, and what she can do with a piece of stiffened material is very impressive. Sometimes the result stands over two feet in all directions.

Meanwhile, down in the main part of the cinema, Nigerian life goes on just the way it goes on in the street. Patrons walk in and out during any part of the film and call out greetings to friends and relatives seated ten rows away, *"Coy-o! Coy-o!"* Others join in. The nasal Binni greeting is less formal than the Hausa, and sounds like children provoking one another. The shoeshine boy makes calls and does his work at the feet of those few patrons who come wearing shoes. Someone unwraps a banana leaf package of *gari*, and it is shared with much noisy lip smacking and sounds of enjoyment. If the film has plenty of color, singing and dancing, and especially fights, the stars are loudly encouraged by their fans. Elvis Presley films and Indian films were particular favorites for their content of what is considered great entertainment in West Africa.

If the film did not deliver the expected amount of action, there was frequently trouble. Many nights Saidi locked himself in the projection room to out wait a crowd which felt entitled to a refund, sometimes after watching the entire movie. There was one occasion when the Indian film didn't follow the usual pattern, and apart from the calvary charge which Saidi had previewed when he chose it, no exciting action ensued. Discontented muttering became angry yelling, and patrons threw their banana skins and other detritus upward in the direction of the projection windows. They were forming into one of those mobs which regularly attacked the projection room, when one patron found a way to resolve his problem and recoup his three and a half shillings.

"*Aha*" he said. "*Dis filum he be never worth t'ree and six. Dis chair, he be worth t'ree and six. Make I go take um.*" With that, he placed the chair on his head in the usual African carrying position, and out he went. He was followed by every other patron in the place, each taking his seat with him.

The next shipment of cinema chairs was bolted to the floor.

I wanted to watch a few Indian films since many were a source of great amusement to the European expats. *Patal Nagri* was my favorite, although I also sat through *Ayee Malinkee Bella* and *Koon Ka Koon*. Like *The Wizard of Oz,* it was perfectly acceptable to have a film in black and white and technicolor. In Indian films, however, if the budget didn't run to color for the whole thing, then just the song and dance episodes would be colored. The heroine always had a ring in her nose and would sing songs about her true love, whom she frequently described as having a face like a full moon. The baddies were never just boring old people, but usually demons and wizards, who at the drop of a hat would turn into prehistoric monsters and fight. I enjoyed these films hugely. So did the Nigerians. I doubt that any of us understood any of them, mind.

After I had been working a couple of months, it was time to visit Lagos, the capital, for some more films. Saidi usually went up and down the hundred and fifty odd miles in a day, but generously offered to take my husband and myself and make a weekend trip out of it.

Anyone visiting the capital was honor bound to announce it at the club, which was the signal for long shopping lists to be made out by all the expatriate ladies. It became obvious that there wasn't going to be much time for anything but work, although it was going to be fun checking out other stores apart from Kingsway and Karo.

My first collection of items to be acquired varied from lavender ric-rac braid to a bottle of cognac. The most important item was a new bikini for me. Life in darkest Africa required an unlimited supply of bikinis and cocktail dresses.

We had to leave by 5:30 a.m., which gave us ample opportunity to enjoy to the full the pinkness of an African morning. Nowhere are mornings so pink and so lovely. This close to the equator it gets light in about fifteen minutes somewhere about 6 a.m., and it gets dark just as abruptly twelve hours later. The dawn is unbelievably gorgeous; the pinkness of it seems to touch the ground around you but it passes while you are still trying to catch your breath. There is no messing about with artificial daylight savings times so you know that dinner will always be eaten after dark, which is somehow very civilized.

The road to Lagos was paved. It was supposed to be wide enough for two vehicles but frequently was worn away at the edges so that traffic careened along in the center. The jungle along the sides of the road was littered with wrecked vehicles, many of them mammy wagons. These lorries, painted gaily in more colors than Joseph's coat, proclaimed *I AM WHAT I AM THANKS GOD* and *TAKE ME PRETTY* and other enigmatic admonitions via signs on the front, back and sides. As many human beings would be squeezed inside as could possibly fit into the space, then more would be stuffed in on top. A few persons hung onto the sides by dint of fingernails and belief in God, and the vehicles would take off on journeys through jungle and bush, frequently in the middle of the road and usually at high speed. There were constantly terrible accidents.

Most lorries seemed to be Mercedes. They must have stood up to the rigors of the road in West Africa better than anything else. They were not immune to breakdowns, however; and on that trip it seemed as though every Mercedes lorry we passed was stopped beside the road with a couple pairs of black legs sticking out of the engine.

We reached Lagos at about 10:00 a.m. It was exotic and exciting-a sprawling shanty town abutting beautiful skyscrapers, gracious expatriate communities with colonial style homes, palm trees and flame trees and traffic and thousands upon thousands of people and the sea!

I hadn't realized how much I had missed the sea. Born and bred in Cornwall at the south-western tip of England, I was never more than

twenty miles from the sea. I caught its scent above even the storm drains
and the perfumed frangipani, and my eyes filled with tears. Saidi was a
soft touch. He hurried his visits to the American Motion Picture
Corporation offices and the Indian film distributor, not waiting for
screening time but just picking out movies by name and description,
(leaving himself open to more disaffected patrons in the future) and drove
us down to Victoria Beach. This is a lovely stretch of shore with white
sand and curving coconut palms. Local fishermen drag their nets through
the water and some Nigerians were sitting around on the beach, chatting
and laughing. Shoes off, I was in the surf immediately. Saidi's admonitions
to watch for the undertow were more than warranted. It was all I could
do to keep my feet in knee-deep water. It was wonderful, mind.

Somehow I was persuaded to pay attention to the shopping lists provided by all those land-bound madames in Benin, and so we sampled the
wonders of Leventis and UTC department stores, and some of the spe-
cialty shops at Lagos' gorgeous international hotels.

Dinner was memorable. The Lebanese owners of *Ciro's* in Apapa were
his old friends, and made peppered steak the way Saidi liked it. The meat
was always imported. Lagosians didn't run out of good meat as often as
those of us in more bush areas. In Africa when you ask for peppered steak
that's what you get, a steak slathered in a hot sauce of peppercorns and
ground black pepper. After that introduction I always ordered peppered
steak when I visited *Ciro's*, and was unbearably disappointed later in life
when I discovered that peppered steak in America meant pieces of meat
and cut up green peppers. The other memorable thing about *Ciro's* was
how dark it was in there. You could hardly find your table again after a
trip to the Ladies' Room.

We stayed in Apapa, the dockside suburb of Lagos, about a mile away
across Lagos Lagoon from the Marina boulevard, because Saidi had
friends in that area. Getting to and from Lagos Island could be something
of a problem as the traffic was always terrible, and the turn at the 7-Up
factory could take you half an hour to negotiate.

Traffic lights in Nigeria were about as much use as the accoutrements unnecessary to the boar hog in the old adage. They were either out, broken, or ignored. I heard there was a time when they were most definitely taken notice of; this when the first light was placed in service in the northern town of Kaduna. The local population turned out in force to watch this spectacular form of entertainment, and the packed crowds snarled traffic completely as they stopped to react to the changing colors with *Oohs* and *Aahs* suitable for a fireworks display.

I hated to leave Lagos. Even the dreadful traffic and mayhem of the Ikorodu Road didn't daunt me. This road leads to the airport and is thus the first impression most visitors have of Nigeria's capital. It isn't a good one. I hear that traffic is worse now, and the journey which used to take an hour now takes a day, and you must pack a cooler in your car with drinks and sandwiches. At that time it was confusion enough, just with the amount of traffic and the blithe disregard for regulations which is the attitude of the average Nigerian. Many feel that it will help matters if they are seen to be impatient, so constant honking and blaring of car horns makes the din unbelievable. To sit on the car roof with one foot through the driver's window pressing continuously on the horn is one way of passing the time during a traffic jam. It seems to unnerve nobody but expats.

Eventually we left the maelstrom that was the Ikeja end of Lagos and entered the race to eternity that was the road back to Benin. There had been a fire in the jungle on our right and in one place a lone tree stood within sight of the road, hollowed out by the fire, with flames from its interior appearing now and again through the opening at the top and the holes where there had once been branches. The rest of the vegetation was entirely blackened. Once it was the custom to burn land to re-energize the soil, but this eventually does more harm than good. The fire could have been set that way, but was more likely accidental since there is little agriculture in the jungle itself. Luckily, it didn't appear to pose a threat to any of the lean-to dwellings in the area.

CHAPTER 11

On May 30, 1967, the Eastern State seceded from the union of Nigerian states under the name of Biafra. The immediate result of this was another curfew. The worst result of this was that Mamadu had to leave work early every evening in order to reach his home before curfew was imposed at sundown.

This curfew was not as much fun as the last since we no longer lived in a block of flats and company was limited. Luckily, there always seemed to be bank staff coming and going on different postings, and it was usual for them to stay at bank accommodations en route. There were therefore often a couple of guests to help liven up the evenings on which we couldn't go to the club.

Rumors abounded as to the reasons for secession. Benin City was not exactly the hub of the universe and did not have the ear of the Premier, but to us the answer was clearly the oil. Nigerian crude was the second purest in the world after Houston, USA, .05% sulfur. At that point in time, almost all of the oil discoveries in Nigeria had been in the eastern area around the delta. It seemed obvious enough that no country could allow the location of its newest, most precious resource to just opt out. Of course, afterwards major oil fields were discovered in many other locations. Warri was one. That scruffy little laterite-dusted village I had visited only a few months previously was destined to become Nigeria's biggest boomtown a decade or so in the future. We heard that Biafra's official reasoning concerned the ongoing tribal differences between the northerners and those living to the south and east. So this was to be another reprisal for the reprisals we had already experienced? Military Governor and self-styled Premier Emeka Ojukwu's action could obviously provoke no other reaction than civil war.

Life went on. We still had a good time and went out at night whenever the curfew was lifted. The expat social life had always included an exhausting round of parties and it would have taken more than a civil war to make us give those up.

At first we confidently expected the war to be over soon, since we took into account the relative sizes of the factions involved. However, it's hard to make soldiers out of cattle herders and tribesmen who have never ridden in an automobile before, let alone had to drive military jeeps through areas where their lifelong enemies may be waiting to do unto them the terrible things which all tribes had been doing to one another for centuries. Then we heard that Biafra had begun hiring mercenaries, and white people mixed up in the conflict gave it a seriousness that we had not heretofore attributed to it. Names of famous mercenaries like Mad Mike Hoare and Rolf Steiner were bandied about in the club. Obviously this promised to be much more than the usual inter-tribal *troubles*. Some American companies began getting a little nervous and started to ship their women and children out. It was a constant source of aggravation to the Europeans that their High Commissions would let them stick it out while the Americans always looked after their own, regardless of cost. Of course, if anyone *had* tried to make us leave the country, we wouldn't have gone.

During one curfew-less period, we were at the club for cinema night. A small, bespectacled Englishman named Tom was sitting on a stool at the bar, chatting with a couple of other Englishmen, who stood around smoking English-pub fashion. The cinema was about fifty feet away through two large open rooms. As always, the Nigerian national anthem preceded the film. Engrossed in conversation, Tom did not hear it. Seconds later, two soldiers dragged him off to prison for not having stood during the national anthem. It was a couple of days before his release could be secured. I felt at the time that this was unnecessarily jumpy on the part of the military, and maybe we should blame it on the war. The experience had been terrible, according to Tom, and he was bitter about being left for two days, unfed, on a bare mud floor at the mercy of rats and cockroaches. We made a mental note: keep on the right side of the military.

Benin had its share of characters and we enjoyed them. There was an ex-Luftwaffe pilot who used to play snooker with us. The table could have doubled as a mini-golf course, it had so many pits; so the quality of play wasn't that good. Whoever lost, he and my husband would hugely enjoy trading insults with World War II overtones. I can still see Herbert laughing wolfishly at my spouse's imprecations of *"Hun swine!"* as the tall German expat potted the black for the third time. A leading Nigerian in the town was also a memorable club-member. He was Tom Ogbe, tall, coal-black and terribly correct as to dress code, who played golf every day clad in plus-fours and argyle socks. His appearance in this dusty, semi-jungle might have made one blink, but he was *au fait* with what was going on and the expats would occasionally try to pump him for information on the war.

Rumor had it that the Biafrans (we still thought of them as *Easterners* and were surprised at the sympathy they seemed to be getting from the rest of the world) were going to break out of the east and take over Benin in its capacity as the capital of the Mid-Western State. It was obviously on their way if they wanted to march on Lagos. The rumors reached more companies, who shipped off their expat women and children, and by now America was calling home its expat males. We were indignant. Many English women were still there, for heaven's sake! Fortunately, at that time of the year most of the expat children were back in England or America at their boarding schools.

My husband and I talked the situation over, and he suggested I go back to the relative safety of the plateau and Jos for a while. The East would surely come through Benin City. Then, after things had died down, I could return. This suited me. Most of our friends had left and life was getting a little quiet, especially since there was *another* curfew. Besides, I couldn't wait to see the plateau again.

So I came back to Jos, and it was as beautiful as ever. I stayed at the bank flats and visited all my old friends. I made the rounds of Lebanese lunches, Syrian dinners, and drank *ahwe-min-hel* (Arabic coffee with cardamom seed) at all times of the day with Middle Eastern friends in the lock-up shops along Ahmadu Bello Street.

My old friends Carole and Ian were off on leave, and I waved them goodbye at the airport together with a batch of drunkards who had tried unsuccessfully to pour Ian onto the plane, since the fact that he didn't care for flying was well known. Carole suggested I take over her job for the duration, since she would like it kept for her return, in case they got posted once more to the plateau. My sojourn should only be for a week or two, but I thought I'd give it a try. This was how I came to be working half days at the back of a perfume factory on Ahmadu Bello Street. My bosses were two Syrian brothers who were always very kind to me and more than generous with their *ahwe-min-hel*, even though cardamom seed was five Nigerian pounds a pound at that time.

Days passed, and weeks. The expected didn't happen. The Biafran troops stayed where they were, and I started to wonder whether I was just having a free holiday. After five weeks, guilt won out and I decided to return to Benin.

Ojo, Benin's Standard Bank driver, came to meet me in our own little green Volkswagen. This was an almost new car which we had purchased from the previous Chief of Police of Benin, who had taken a posting to another part of Nigeria. We had to drive fast from the airport because of the 7:00 p.m. curfew. At 7:02 p.m., we hurtled up to a road block on the outskirts of Benin. It was manned by a couple of businesslike soldiers who were giving a hard time to the two drivers ahead of mine. Still accustomed to being deferred to because of my color, I could hardly believe it when they also refused to let me through. I looked around at the looming jungle, the disgruntled occupants of the vehicles ahead and those which were drawing up behind me, and swatted a mosquito which dive-bombed us through the open car window. I was going to have to spend the night out here, obviously. Poor Ojo had to contend with the gear lever. At least I had the back seat.

I was born lucky. Before I had time to properly put my feet up, a military jeep screeched up to the barrier, on the wrong side of the road. A tall, imposing young soldier alighted. He was wearing some badges of rank but I don't know his rank because I have never learned to differentiate between them. He peered into each vehicle in the queue and grunted with satisfaction when he saw me.

"Come here!" he called to a pretty girl who was sitting in his jeep. He turned to me. "Madame, this my wife. Please take her to my house in Benin City. Thank you."

She got in beside me and he waved Ojo out into the other lane and past the soldiers guarding the barrier. It was strange to be riding in that quiet city, where usually the traffic roared until early morning and the roads were full of people. We located her house easily and she got out, calling a cheerful good night. The next part was hairy, getting to the bank, because we had no proof that it was OK for us to be riding around after curfew and the penalty, getting shot on sight, applied to all persons of all races. We made it without incident.

The nightwatch was asleep. Some things never change. Since the curfews he almost never got woken up any more. Of course, I didn't have my key. I ascended the back steps and kicked my foot at the door with all my strength. The door burst inward. A startled lizard fell on my head, and disentangling itself from my hair it completed its fall to the floor and scuttled busily away. My husband was asleep in a chair in the sitting room. Door noises no longer woke him. He probably dreamed I was a bank inspector. Home again.

CHAPTER 12

The first rain of the season is an exciting event. The smell is overwhelming. All over town, people rush out to their balconies and verandahs and sniff and hold out their hands. It smells so good! The scent of rain is instantly recognizable, even if one has never consciously smelled water before. There is instinctive understanding of how horses and other animals can scent it.

The red dust settles, the vegetation shines. After a short time the shower stops, the sun returns, and the roads steam. There may not be another shower for over a month. Finally it rains again, then again, and the showers get harder and closer together until it's the month of July and God empties His celestial bath water almost without ceasing for four or five weeks. Gradually the sunny intervals get longer, the flooded roads and storm drains recoup their individual delineations, and another dry season is on its way.

In Nigeria, the greens of the golf courses consist of dark brown sand, not grass, and are therefore referred to as browns, not greens. In the rainy season the browns may not even be visible under flooding, so nobody cares if the brown sand becomes mud. If it's under a foot and a half of water you can't play anyway. During the rains the laterite becomes mud and many roads become impassable.

It had been expected that the Biafran troops would get on with seizing Benin City en route to attacking Lagos just as soon as the rains had subsided enough to make the roads passable. I had only been back from Jos five days when they came through.

The takeover was a masterpiece of bloodless military strategy. My experience was slightly different from that of most people, since I was one of only two expatriates who did not get captured on that first morning.

August 9th began with a quite unprecedented happening, which in itself should have made me uneasy. Mamadu didn't turn up. We later learned that soldiers had rounded up everyone they found on the streets and sent them back home. It therefore fell to me to make some coffee, and I took a cup downstairs to my breakfastless spouse at work in the bank offices. As I went back up the outside steps to the flat, I could see a soldier running alongside a building opposite, coming towards me in the direction of the bank. His furtive manner attracted my attention, but he didn't see me. His rifle was held at the ready; but then, the military were everywhere since there was a war on, and they all seemed to like to play with their guns. It was quite usual to see soldiers loosing rounds of bullets upwards into the air for no reason other than apparent high spirits.

The apartment windows were open on all sides and I could look down on the five laterite roads which met in this main part of town. Everything was strangely quiet. There was no traffic. I could see only one regular pedestrian and that was the young paper boy who used to sell the *Daily Times*, Nigeria's foremost newspaper, on an opposite corner. A soldier was pushing him around, and as I watched, the boy's papers were snatched away from him and thrown down into the mud. The soldier stomped them into illegibility and motioned the young boy to take off.

The lack of usual cacaphony and traffic, and the absence of my dependable Mamadu, finally convinced me that something was wrong. I picked up the phone to call downstairs to the bank. No dial tone. One of our house guests joined me. He was passing through on transfer and was some-one I knew from the bank flats in Jos. His family had never joined in the usual expat frivolities as they were of a missionary bent, and spent a lot of time singing hymns with any of the locals they could persuade to take part. His wife kept a steward whose primary occupation was to wipe off door handles with the British standby disinfectant named Dettol. Since I used unfiltered water to brush my teeth, ate everything which didn't get out of my way, hadn't bought Dettol since U.K., and was rewarded with rude good health and a lack of tummy palaver which earned me the nickname of *Iron Guts*, I had never really had anything in common with her. Our interaction had therefore been limited to the occasional smile and wave.

House-guest and I decided that something unusual was definitely going on, and in case we might have to do some escaping into bush at some point, we felt we ought to change into serviceable trousers and shoes; espe-cially me, as I was in my usual miniskirt. We had a very nebulous idea of what we were actually going to do in any given situation, mind you. My guest was inordinately grateful that I wasn't going to panic. "My wife would scream," he kept telling me.

For almost two hours we sat on the floor below the field of vision afforded by the open windows, occasionally bobbing up and down to see if anything was going on in the streets. Eventually the men returned in jeeps filled with soldiers and machine guns. They came upstairs and told their story.

We had been taken over by Biafra. In order to fool anyone seeing them before their takeover was complete, the soldiers had removed their Biafran rising sun insignia. The major communications and commerce centers of the town had been hit simultaneously: ECN, the Post Office, the radio sta-tion, banks, etc., and all telephone lines had been cut. The personnel from these organizations had been rounded up at gun point and herded onto the large grassy roundabout near Kingsway, where Biafran commanders had informed them at machine-gun-point that the operation was a complete success, that we should consider the Mid-West occupied territory, and that we should behave, carry on business as usual, and observe a curfew from sunset to sunrise.

"Oh, not *again!*" I wailed.

I was also disappointed that nobody had seen any mercenaries.

Apart from the inconvenience of eating dinner at 4:30 p.m. so that Mamadu could leave in time to reach home before sundown (God forbid they shot a steward of such excellence!) the takeover period wasn't too bad. We all got a little sick of having our every move covered by machine guns, however.

The biggest machine gun post in town was on the huge roundabout next to Kingsway. Hardly surprising. Everybody knew that the first order of business during any kind of troubles was to go to Kingsway. That's where all the action would be for a day or two. All the madames promptly descended on the store and bought out the meat department. This was one occasion when nobody needed to prompt anybody else, even if the phones had been working. No-one could guess how long it would be until the next load of food got through, so we would all simply load up with as much as we could afford or find available at the time. That was my largest ever chop purchase. I somehow found room in the fridge and the larder for over one hundred Nigerian pounds' worth of food.

Of course, there was a run on the bank. Even during business as usual, the average African doesn't expect to wait calmly in line until it's his turn. He will usually figure that the squeaky wheel will get the grease and will yell and gesticulate so violently that his neighbor feels forced to outdo him in case of getting overlooked.

Remember that the bank was on its own little plot of land in the center of town. It was an old building without air-conditioning and with open windows on all four sides, and two doors. There was such pandemonium from downstairs that I ventured down the outside steps to see what was going on. The customers were pushing in both doors so determinedly that others already inside were getting pushed out through the windows. They would then race around to the doors and shove their way back in again, dislodging some more, who would in turn fall backwards through the windows. Everyone was very vocal about the situation.

Eventually the patience of my long-suffering spouse wore out. He stood in the center of the banking floor and bawled "SHADDUP!!!!" at the top of his voice. The decibel level lowered to a mere roar. Business as usual.

Living in occupied territory put a damper on social life. The hassle of continual roadblocks lessened daily visiting back and forth, and on my trips to the club I could find nobody there to play with anyway. As far as we were aware, there were only about sixty expats left in the Benin area and the surrounding bush.

During this time, we all formed a very jaundiced view regarding the advisability of freedom of the press. I still adhere to this view. The radio broadcast the news of a large shipment of arms from Britain to the Federal troops in Nigeria. Rumor had it that this incensed our captors to the point that it seemed a good idea to kill us in reprisal. Personally, I had had it with reprisals of any sort. On the other hand, if I could have visited a personal reprisal on the BBC twit who read that out while a bunch of his compatriots were stewing at the mercy of the Federal troops' enemies, I would have grabbed the chance.

With few diversions, I became less inclined to get up early over the following days. At the weekend was in my negligee at mid-morning, freshly washed hair still wet, when I received a telephone call from the wife of the bank manager with the news of our imminent evacuation.

"The High Commission says we are going to Lagos on Sunday (August 13th.) You may each take only one suitcase with you and you are going to have to carry it yourself." (Unheard of!) "Crate your household effects as best you can and label them. They'll be collected and stored after the war. Buses will take us to Sapele where we'll pick up a boat."

At such times, a steward as good as Mamadu was a godsend. Overseeing gardeners and drivers huffing and puffing around with crates, and starting to wrap artwork and linens, he was my savior. I took the precaution of writing him a glowing reference in case we weren't returned to this posting, but made him promise to come back to us if we were.

"Never fear, madame," he said comfortingly.

Twelve brave, admirable, not to mention fool-hardy, men decided to stay behind to oversee the expat business interests and personal cars, etc. The rest of us packed our one permitted suitcase each and were put on a bus for the thirty mile journey to Sapele. There was a misty farewell to those who had volunteered to remain in Benin. None of us dreamed it would be more than two months before we saw them again.

The evacuation taught me a lot, and Rule One is: to elicit the greatest comfort out of the situation, don't look like a refugee just because you are one. I discovered this singular truth by accident. I had had trouble cramming my extensive wardrobe into my one oversized suitcase, so I left all my not-so-glamorous clothing behind for Mamadu. He must have looked a sight for sore eyes for the next couple of months! I ended up wearing a leopard-print mini-dress and high heels. High heeled shoes take up more room in a suitcase than Bata flip-flops, and I had had to have Mamadu sit on the case to fasten it as it was. I wasn't going to leave my favorite shoes behind so I simply decided to wear them and put up with any resultant inconvenience. (There was none.) The other wives, feeling that if you were a refugee then it was appropriate to wear trousers, flat shoes and head scarves, were not amused when an eager young German seaman rushed down the gangplank of the waiting freighter *Steinhoft* at Sapele, and carried my bursting suitcase up onto the ship for me. Of course, everyone else was carrying his or her own, as per instructions.

Mrs. Bell, the wife of the District High Commissioner, was given the Captain's cabin. Otherwise, there were no available seats on the ship but one, held by an officer at the head of the gangplank who was overseeing the evacuation. He stood, saluted, and offered it to me. I didn't dare take it and indicated the glowering visage of the nearby bank manager's wife, who was aware of her seniority to me in both rank and age and had already remarked acidly on my lack of appropriate refugee clothing.

The *Steinhoft* was a German cargo vessel which happened to be docked at Sapele at that critical time. Ropes had been slung approximately two thirds of the way across its length, and Nigerians were being escorted to one end, expatriates to another. There looked to be several hundred Nigerians, and the expat count was about sixty.

Saidi caught up with us. Although not registered with any embassy or high commission, several expatriates of other nationalities had joined the buses or found rides to the dock.

There was no food aboard the ship, but there was beer. It was a German vessel, after all. Most of the male refugees did not find it a hardship cruise. Those of us who didn't like beer and couldn't find a cup of coffee soon decided we might as well sleep the time away. We went below decks to what must have been a cargo hold and made up a cozy little camp by enclosing a space about six foot square within our upright suitcases. Saidi returned from a foraging expedition around the ship carrying a couple of reed mats, which we placed on the floor. I promptly lay down and went to sleep. Apparently the bank manager's wife who had not taken too kindly to me being offered the ship's only chair visited during the night, and was equally put out to discover that I could sleep like a baby during an evacuation. This afforded great amusement to the guys in the immediate vicinity, some of whom were bank employees who had come into contact with her sharp tongue in former days. They wouldn't let her disturb me.

I awoke early and made my way to the deck. The pre-dawn darkness was chilly and the lovely African dawn was marred by showers. I started to sniffle with the beginnings of a cold. The palm trees on either side of the river dipped in that forlorn way palm trees have when they are being rained on. The milk-chocolate colored water slopped over the banks and dripped from the mangroves. As the light brightened, the boat's wake became visible. Small dark shapes bobbing about in it could soon be distinguished as empty beer bottles. Others came sailing down through the air from the upper deck as I watched.

We came to the mouth of the river. A federal gunboat was lying in wait, its guns trained on our decks and its crew looking anything but friendly. There was an exchange of shouts. Like a ripple across a pond the word raced around the ship.

"They want to shoot us!"

"Why!?"

"We just came out of enemy held territory so we might be enemies."

The gunboat didn't move. The *Steinhoft* didn't move. Mrs. Bell did. As befitted her station as High Commissioner's wife she was having breakfast in the Captain's cabin. I noticed that she hadn't even had time to finish dressing as she floated regally by in her robe. The captain of the gunboat and a couple of his henchmen were summoned aboard for a consultation in the cabin with our captain and Mrs. Bell. The guns on the gunboat never moved, but we all felt safer looking down their barrels as long as their boss had the same view. After a while the boarding party emerged. There seemed to be a certain amount of goodwill involved. One of the soldiers passed quite close to me. He was carrying a pail over which a napkin had been carelessly draped. The bucket was definitely filled with bottles.

The boarders returned to their own boat, which backed away and turned, swiveling the guns in another direction. They looked good that way.

We resumed our journey. Now we were going down alongside the coast to Lagos. Not long afterwards, word passed around the ship. We had been ransomed by a dash of three bottles of imported booze. Two whisky and a brandy, they thought.

Relief was tempered by dented egos. Is that all we're worth?

We docked at Apapa, Lagos' dock area. Everyone descended on the Excelsior Hotel for some very welcome coffee and a long overdue meal, which had to make up for breakfast and the dinner we had missed the previous night. I was sneezing continually by now, and my nose was running like the proverbial tap. It's total bathos when all you have to show for being evacuated and held up by an unfriendly gunboat is a bad cold.

~~~

At the time, we were confident that we were the last expats to leave the interior, apart from the twelve men who had volunteered to remain in Benin City. Years later, I discovered that we were wrong.

The Peace Corps was very much a presence in Africa during those years, as were British VSO's (Voluntary Service Overseas.) Because they usually lived out in bush and their lives were not nearly as hedonistic as ours, we knew most of them only slightly or not at all. They took their jobs very seriously, and made a big difference in the lives of many Africans.

Following the military takeover, the PCV's (Peace Corps Volunteers) who were stationed in bush around the Mid-West continued their normal duties and began to have trouble finding food and cigarettes, as these items started to become scarcer. As mentioned before, American companies had already sent home all of their employees and their families. The American Embassy in Lagos had sent some lorries to Benin to pick up Peace Corps personnel but by the time the last four staff members arrived out of the eastern states with their baggage, the lorries and luggage had to remain behind in enemy-held territory.

On August 16th, three days after the *Steinhoft* had left, Lagos radioed urgently that all Volunteers and staff should withdraw immediately from the Midwest. Those personnel remaining boarded buses with a few days' supply of food and water and headed for Sapele. They spent an uncomfortable night in the Sapele Club trying to sleep on the floor and the snooker tables. Next morning, the remaining 74 PCV's, together with eleven staff and few other expats, met their evacuation craft at the dock. And what a craft! They were crowded onto a long, flat, rusty barge, pushed by a tug. They spent 18 hours on this barge-with the only available facilities being a toilet on the tug. Since the vessel had no proper lights, it was forced to lie to at the river's edge overnight, with the passengers totally at the mercy of the ravenous Nigerian mosquitoes. According to one survivor, the only bright spot was the occasional nip from one of the few bottles stashed in the personal baggage down in the hold.

They were met at Escravos, where the river meets the ocean, by the *Niger Tide*. This was a Gulf Oil owned scow, which came complete with hot coffee and a meal. *That* beat our gunboat episode, at least! They finally reached Lagos at 8 a.m. on the Sunday morning, after a night washed by waves breaking over the deck, and not a dry place to sleep. One PCV lost his pet monkey on the trip, but otherwise, everyone lived to tell the tale...and also to lament the inability to complete the projects which many of them had labored over for up to eighteen months.

CHAPTER 13

There was much speculation as to whether we would get sent back to U.K. for an early leave, but we were absorbed into the Apapa staff for the next three months. This suited me. Any time I could stay in Nigeria it suited me. Also the rains were ending and I could get back to pool-lying, a sport that I could easily have taken to the Olympics.

So it was that I read every book in the Apapa Club while turning slowly as if on a spit, and rolling off the edge of the pool into the tepid water every hour or so. From the window of our newly-assigned flat, where I daily checked on the satisfactory darkening of my own hide, I could see a large billboard extolling the effects of Artra skin lightening cream. This unguent was meanwhile being used in great quantities by the indigenous population to try to look like I did before I started trying to look like them. It takes all sorts.

Our new steward was Thomas. He wasn't bad. Since I never thought to see another Mamadu I think I didn't expect much of Thomas to start with; plus, our household effects were not with us-*again*-and so he had very little with which to work. There were some nice restaurants in the Apapa area, and the nightclub at the Excelsior Hotel was excellent, so we ate out a lot. The *Safari* restaurant opened up under Lebanese proprietorship and

I developed such a liking for Lebanese *fattouche* salad that I was perfectly happy to go there regularly and have it for appetizer, entree, and dessert.

Thomas did make great stuffed onions. One night he was wincing as he served them, and as his stomach was aching I gave him some antacid pills and sent him home. He frequently said he wasn't well and finally succumbed to my nagging to see a doctor. I felt that his idea of a doctor and mine probably differed, and never was convinced that he didn't just go to the local *juju-man*. A few months later, when we returned from leave, I learned that Thomas had died of cancer of the stomach.

This sad event at least delivered him from my verbal opinion of his packing. I had not wanted to go on leave and had ignored the date, hoping that it would go away. It didn't. We had had to attend one of many going-away parties at lunch time on our last day, and at that point I had to admit I was hopelessly behind in the crating of our household effects. I had asked Thomas to complete the job. Three months later on our return we discovered that he had duly packed the kettle and the coffeepot still filled with water and coffee respectively.

I enjoyed my time in Apapa, although I preferred the Ikoyi end of Lagos because I had always liked the Ikoyi Club so much. Lagos was on a series of islands joined by bridges and causeways. In the middle was Lagos Island, the location of all major businesses. It was joined to the east by Ikoyi Island, where most expats lived in modern and colonial homes amid straight streets and landscaped yards. Ikoyi was joined to Victoria Island by a bridge across Five Cowrie Creek, and Victoria Island was where most of the new building was going on in the days of the civil war. Getting to Apapa meant leaving Lagos Island at the north western end and crossing the small island of Iddo to the mainland, then doubling back towards the south. It was much faster in a boat. If one didn't turn off left at Iddo towards Apapa but carried on northwards one would come to the mainland at Ebute-Metta. This was the area always referred to as *the Mainland*. What with Lagos Lagoon, the harbor, Five Cowrie Creek, Porto Novo Creek, Badagri Creek, and the bay entitled the Bight of Benin, there was water, water everywhere. Looking down from a plane, I used to wonder where they found space to put all the buildings.

The beaches were beautiful. The only thing I liked better than a pool was a beach. To the south of Apapa and to the east of Victoria Island across the harbor mouth was Tarkwa Bay, sheltered by moles running either side. At Tarkwa you could water-ski and swim, and then walk across the mole to the glorious 500-mile length of Lighthouse Beach where the waves always crashed in an endless invitation to come surfing.

The weeks were wonderful and the weekends were heaven. After a Saturday night's cocktails, dinner, then dancing till dawn, we would swap cocktail dresses for bikinis and shorts, grab a towel and a book, and drive over to *Fred's Place*. *Fred's Place* was our fond contraction for the *Federal Palace Hotel*. This gorgeous great, modern hotel with a lobby the size of Dahomey was located on Victoria Island. A path meandered from the hotel through a garden of lovely hybrid hibiscus blossoms to a rickety wooden dock, from which rickety wooden *banana boats* left every half hour for the beach at Tarkwa Bay. The banana boats were the marine equivalent of mammy wagons. Consisting of collections of parallel plank seats over none-too-watertight hulls, inadequately covered by roofs mainly of dried paint flakes in several primary colors, these things were the recognized public transport to the beach island. They were all propelled by ancient 30 h.p. Johnson engines, which had doubtless been rejected by Noah as too old for his needs. Stuffed to the gills with sweating foreigners, the banana boats would chug backwards and forwards all day on Saturdays, Sundays, and whatever Christian and Moslem religious holidays turned up.

If we got there early enough, we could sit on *Fred's Place* terrace, a large terrazzo expanse overlooking the hibiscus and the bougainvillea, and order a delicious breakfast of fresh pressed orange juice and napoleons. (The *Fred's Place* pastry chef was a wizard at napoleons.) Then we'd catch the 8:30 a.m. ferry. At night that terrace was one of the nicest places in Lagos to sit because of the large amount of jasmine vines climbing up the outside from the ground floor. The scent was heavenly.

On reaching the beach island, there was a small walk from another rickety wooden dock through a grassy area to the back of the beach. The back edge of the beach was lined with palm huts joined together like English terraced houses. Every so often, there would be a break to allow access to the company beach houses, which were set back among the casuarina trees. I always took one of the semi-detached huts at the end of a row. The boys who supervised the huts were quick to recognize a good customer and it wasn't long before 'my' hut was always reserved for me. We would also give a small dash for a couple of reed mats that we could place on the hot sand outside to lie on.

It was a laid back lifestyle at the beach. We would arrange ourselves horizontally and go to sleep in the sun. After a while we would wake up and turn over, then go to sleep again. I could keep this up for hours, particularly since I almost never slept on a Saturday night, and sometimes danced so many hours that my feet still hurt on Tuesday.

Many vendors of fruit and drinks plied the beaches. They all carried their heavy enamel trays on their heads and called out as they passed.

"Orange? Nice orange. Get pineapple! Cheap-cheap!"

"How much?" someone would say. That was the signal for the vendor to kneel on the sand, put down the tray, and extol the virtues of the greeny-yellow oranges or the great, golden Nigerian pineapples. Many of the vendors were small girls. They could not have been old enough to go to school. I was not good at estimating children's ages as I had none of my own, but I knew expat kids of two years who were the same size. One solemn little girl in particular would come by. I would point to her oranges and ask for a price.

"Is two-twopence, madame," she would reply.

"What? Two-twopence?" I would make noises indicative of cardiac arrest. "Make I give you penny-penny," I would offer. She wouldn't crack a smile.

"Is two-twopence, madame." She knew she had me. I might be able to halve the price of an orange from an adult vendor from twopence to a penny apiece, but the kid was so cute! Of course, mother knew this when she sent out her offspring in the first place. Then the child would begin to peel the fruit with a knife whose wickedness we would never let within a mile of an expat kid of twice that age. She was good, too. As I have said, Nigerian oranges aren't the fat, orange ones which Florida churns out in such great abundance. They are, however, great juice oranges. The usual way to enjoy one is to peel away the outside of the skin, leaving a white, pith covered sphere. A small plug in the shape of a cone is cut from the top where the stem used to be, and then the juice is sucked out of the hole, with the fruit being squeezed simultaneously until it is a wrung-out blob. In most of my beach photos from that time the whitish blob of an orange obscured the lower part of my face.

The pineapples were more expensive but no less juicy. They were so large that you needed a few accomplices to help eat them. After all, there was no handy place to put down the remains to be picked up later. One day, humming the Pat Boone song *Love Letters in the Sand*, we were waiting for a vendor to finish hacking the skin from a particularly large pineapple. Salivating, I passed slices out to each of my friends. I took the last slice, and dropped it. Without missing a beat, several rugby-club trained voices sang,

"Day after day, We pass the time away, Dropping pineapples in the sand."

Personally, I didn't think it was funny. I had to make do with a tepid Fanta orange soda from one of the native stands.

For a shilling you could rent a surf board from the collection at the back of Lighthouse Beach and keep the thing the rest of the day if you liked. They were only body boards-the large, malibu type of board had reached Europe by then, but not all of the colonies. Nevertheless, we had a great deal of fun with those boards. The surf on Lighthouse Beach was not as regular as on Cornwall's north coast, but it was a lot more reliable since it never died down. I lost hours just hurtling in, getting up, plodding back, zooming in, getting up, plodding back, etc. etc. Due to the warmth of the water in that climate, there was never a need to get out because of being cold. Eventually, I would realize that I was tired and had been in some kind of daze for a long time. (The lack of Saturday night sleep was doubtless the main contributor to my lost Sunday hours.)

There were always friends on the beach; friends you knew, not just the hopeful males who followed you down the beach inviting you to everything from their beach house to the Caledonian Ball. Some comrades would hail from the shade of a palm tree and ply you with pink gins. Others would invite you to water-ski, join a picnic or come sailing. There was always a party going on in this or that beach house, and always a fairly rowdy mob celebrating living over a greasy lunch of eggs and bacon fried in groundnut oil at the beach bar. The beach was like our life in cameo, fun taken so seriously that the worst care was a hangover, or maybe a bit too much sun.

Towards the end of the afternoon, mats would be returned, final dashes would change hands, and the red-striped revelers would again trudge over the grass to the dock. By the time the banana boat had done its work the tables in the Federal Palace gardens would look very inviting, and we would sit and drink fresh-pressed orange juice and Star beer and watch the other sun-wearied fun seekers disembark. Usually they would join us, and a table for six would become a table of nineteen, and the path of those trying to find their way straight from dock to car park would meander even further among the hibiscus blossoms. It was hell on the Coast.

Sunday was the steward's usual day off. We almost never took food to the beach so dinner would loom large in our minds by the time we finally reached home again. A shower, a hair wash, a generous lathering of Astral cream (no, not Artra!) on sunburned flesh, and a couple of hours later everyone would be in the *Safari* at an oversized table filled with *fattouche*, *kafta*, and garlic-laden *hummus*.

~~~

We enjoyed three months of this, enough for my tan to please even me, then had to go on leave. The usual tour was eighteen months, then three and a half months' leave. Senior managers would do ten and two. We were given an early leave so its duration was only about three months.

Only? That was more than enough! The best bit was where we spent a week staying with our old friends in Jos on the way. We had to refute a few slanders about Lagos while there. A strange couple recently transferred from Lagos had told people the weather was so hot there that nobody went out until after 5:30 in the evening, but just stayed home in the air conditioning. Our tans disproved that one.

The rest of the leave was downhill all the way. We had imagined that our old drinking buddies, and everyone else for that matter, would be enthralled at our adventures. No way were we prepared for the lack of interest in our new, improved, exciting lifestyle, nor the total involvement our old friends exhibited in continuing with the same old blah stuff that they had been doing for decades.

Then there was the food problem. No *hummus*. Worse, no curry. Worst of all-you had to get it yourself. We tried eating out a lot but ran out of money, and in any case, the food was boring. We crossed off a lot of days on a lot of calendars. We bought a lot of clothes, mostly thin shirts, cocktail dresses and bikinis. We left Cornwall a week early when the hundred years of exile was finally coming to a close, and visited some ex-Benin friends in Kent. That improved matters a bit. Not only did they want to talk about Nigeria but they wanted to talk about all their U.K. friends *not* wanting to talk about Nigeria. We could identify with that. Unfortunately their company was not sending them back to Nigsville. We'd miss them, supposing we returned to Benin. (Actually we were praying for Lagos.)

The final days we spent in London, and paid a couple of visits to the downstairs bar at *Snow's* of Piccadilly, where Old Coasters are wont to gather when they are exiled to U.K. We met some and felt better. We partied with them for several hours and felt better still. Finally we left, promising to get together with them in Africa as soon as they returned from leave, and made our joyous way to the airport.

It was February, and as we turned the corner to the Victoria terminal, London hurled one of those icy blasts of wind at us, the kind which hurts your throat and turns your legs blue. It was England's way of saying good-bye. Never mind. We had the last laugh. We were clutching our tickets to the sun.

CHAPTER 14

You may remember those twelve men who volunteered to stay behind in occupied territory when the rest of us were evacuated. The course of the war did not go well for Biafra and the Biafrans did not march on Lagos as planned. Their hold on the Mid-West weakened. After two months it was determined by the powers that be in Lagos, the High Commission and the Embassies representing those citizens involved, and their employers, that it was time to go and get the heroes. They had a lot of stories to tell.

The guys had been very busy at first. All the expats' cars which had been left behind were jacked up and the wheels removed. This prevented their being commandeered as military vehicles. The twelve stayed together where possible, in one expat house after another. Because of the usual rush to Kingsway which had taken place just before evacuation, all the houses had full fridges. They would stay at a house until its food was finished, then move. They checked out the crating of the remaining expat belongings and made sure that articles which might tempt a looting soldier were out of sight. Business wound down as many of the population had been evacuated and supply lines were cut off.

The twelve spent their evenings together at whatever amusements they could find. This included one of them playing a trumpet in bed, which did not endear him to his roommate. They took over the local cinema and played every copy of every film in stock. During the time when the Federal troops were trying to retake Benin, the friends were gathered in the cinema watching *The Longest Day*. This is a war film with plenty of sound effects.

There was a polite knock on the door. It was a Biafran soldier with a message from his commander, "Please sah, turn down de filum. We cannot hear the enemy!"

Roadblocks became more ubiquitous and more of a nuisance. They were set up at short intervals on every traversable road. One day, our Swiss friend Frank was driving his car with his doberman in the back seat. The dog was large and mean and had been trained as a watchdog. It didn't like anyone to look askance at its master. They stopped at a roadblock. A soldier jammed his rifle through the driver's window and snapped at Frank, "Get out and be searched!"

The dog, assuming a threat to its master, lunged partially out of the back window with a bare-toothed growl.

"Ah!" yelped the soldier, totally losing his cool. "Get out and search yourself!"

The strain of their position told on the twelve; and their provisions dwindled. During the last two weeks of their stay in Benin City, their meals consisted mainly of eggs and yam chips. The men said they never wanted to see either again. They all lost weight. One, a bank manager, became sick and was very ill by the time he was returned to us in Lagos.

There was one final foul-up. Two of the twelve coincidentally happened to be named A. Colquhoun. Since this is not the most common of names, the High Commission assumed it to be a typo and sent a helicopter to pick up eleven men. They were all eventually airlifted out, brought to Lagos, duly thanked, examined, and sent home on leave.

Those of us who had left our belongings behind also had cause to thank them as we lost nothing. Even our cars were intact (once we had had the wheels reattached.)

Word came down from bush that an expat named Steve Stephens, whom we understood to be a teacher with the Peace Corps, had been summarily shot by the Biafrans for refusing to allow them to commandeer his car. If the story were true, then that is the only expat casualty of the Nigerian Civil War which has come to my attention.

There very nearly was another one, though. This is where my friend Sandie comes in. We didn't meet until several years later in Florida, where we swapped war stories and laughed together over being on opposite sides.

Sandie is six feet of va-va-voom English redhead. At the time, she had the same measurements as Raquel Welch, equally impressively distributed. In addition, she had more than her fair share of brain power *and* a sense of humor. I always felt I really should have hated that kind of competition. An ex-Bluebell Girl, (England's version of the *Rockettes,)* her varied career had led her to be the only female in the world selling commercial aircraft.

Biafra was in a war. Biafra needed fighter aircraft. Sandie was selling them. So far, so good.

The day came when she and a pilot delivered a two-seater Fouga Magister trainer to Sao Tome airport for the Biafrans. The rest is in her own words....

I could see a small reception committee waiting for us. We taxied to the side of the group and stopped. Peter, my associate, climbed out of the cockpit and gave me a hand. Colonel Ojukwu and his Chief Minister greeted me whilst Pete showed the Biafran Chief Pilot over the fighter plane.

"We'll leave those two, Sandra, and escort you to your hotel," said the Colonel.

"But I thought I was returning immediately to Lisbon on the Red Cross flight," I said. "Now that the trainer has arrived safely, all I need is your signature on these papers."

"Sorry, my dear. We are keeping you here until the rest of the aircraft arrive." The Colonel said this with a disarming smile.

"But that's another three or four days-and I don't even have a change of clothes!"

The minister took my elbow and steered me towards Customs. "You have no choice," he said, "So you might as well make the best of it."

An officer stamped my passport and handed it to my escort, who immediately pocketed it. "I'll return this as soon as full delivery is made," he said.

It was pointless to argue. We crossed to the jeep where Pete and the Colonel awaited us. After a bumpy ride on a dirt track masquerading as a road we reached a hotel. It was a ramshackle three-story building. I was given a room one floor up. It contained a single bed and a mosquito net full of holes. A cracked washbasin stood in one corner and there was a three-legged wardrobe at the end of the bed, the legless corner being propped up by paperback books. I tried turning on the tap. No surprise. They were for decoration only.

I sat on the edge of the bed closed in by the hopelessness of the situation. I was scared stiff and had to get away, but how? One small airfield. No telephones. Communication was only by radio link to the Colonel's HQ in Lisbon. That was no good to me.

I set out to find Pete and talk things over, and found a massive Biafran guarding my door. He escorted me to Pete's room. Pete de Zeeuw was a gentle giant of a Dutchman. He was going to help train the Biafran pilots in their fight for independence from the Nigerians. Pete's advice was to stick it out; and he loaned me some of his clothes to boost my non-existent wardrobe.

Three days and nights passed in an increasing nightmare. I was not allowed to join Pete at the airport and was confined to the hotel and grounds, which were about a quarter acre of bushes at the edge of the jungle. I was bitten extensively by mosquitoes. My room was alive with cockroaches. And not one aircraft had arrived. Sinister rumors started to circulate and my fear mounted. What would they do with me if the aircraft didn't arrive? On the fourth morning the question was answered. The Colonel said he planned to take me to the women's prison in Biafra by boat in 48 hours.

That evening we had the usual inedible meal. Afterwards, as usual, Pete kissed my hand as he said goodnight. He pressed a small object into my palm and I curled my middle fingers around it.

Back in my room, I examined the object in my hand. It was a tightly folded piece of paper. On it was written, "Rescue tonight 1 a.m. Knot sheets, anything, and wait."

I quietly knotted all the bed linen and secured one end to the ceiling fan. I tested my weight on it, blew out the gaslight, and waited. An interminable time passed during which I responded to every variety of bird call from the jungle. Suddenly some earth was thrown through my window.

"Throw out the rope and climb down. I'll catch you if you fall!" a shadowy figure whispered through the darkness. I threw out the sheets, clambered over the sill and started downwards. It always looked so easy in the movies, but fear made me agile.

My rescuer was an Englishman. He was blacked up with mud. He blackened my face as I struggled into a camouflage overall he had brought with him.

"Follow me. We have to step lively back to the airfield. Don't say a word." As if I would! "I know the whereabouts of most of the guards, but keep your eyes peeled," he instructed.

We weaved around bushes and trees, keeping well away from the dirt road. As we approached the airfield, my knight in camouflage stopped.

"See the Connie over there?" He pointed to the battered Constellation aircraft sitting at the edge of the runway. "I've left the passenger hatch slightly open. Once we reach the grass verge, run as fast as you can and haul yourself in. Close the hatch behind you. I shall be going for the hatch nearest the cockpit."

He had purposely parked the aircraft so that the hatch doors faced away from the lighting on the airport building. We crawled on our bellies through the grass, eyeing the armed men guarding the airport perimeter. My heart raced and my knees and elbows were bleeding. We were so near!

"NOW!" came the harsh order. I was startled into action. I just upped and ran. There was shouting and I could hear shots, so I weaved my way to the hatch. The opening was just above my head, but I jumped and made it first time.

The first engine roared with power.

"Close the damned door!" a voice yelled. It was heavy and very stiff, but I managed it as we started to taxi. The Connie lifted off in an incredibly short length of runway and we were safely on our way to Lisbon.

The problems awaiting there due to lack of passport and aircraft payments were enough for another story.

CHAPTER 15

Getting back from leave was not as easy as it should have been, owing to the weather. February in Nigeria is just beautiful; not so in England. Ice on the runway diverted all flights from landing for about 36 hours, and nothing was able to take off. The dreary weather report discouraged hanging about at the airport so we stayed at the home of a friend who was still in Lagos. His parents made us welcome but the gloom of another cold night was hard to dispel, and they were out of extra blankets, and I couldn't sleep. With my extreme phobia for cold I had been dreaming of no more misery for eighteen months, and I put up with another day of it with very bad grace.

The following day we returned to hanging around Heathrow airport, and eventually a Sabena flight took off. It was going vaguely in the right direction so we got on with the intention of changing planes a few times over warmer parts of Europe. It was without question the worst flight I have ever taken and I am not at all nervous about flying. I should have been grateful to the pilot for taking off at all when nobody else felt like it, but he landed on one wheel with such a jolt that I was hit by a briefcase which left its owner several seats behind me. We ended up on a BOAC VCIO which was aimed at Lagos and by this time we were tired and more out of sorts than ever. Plane seats are scientifically designed to render sleep impossible if you are a female of 5 feet 9 1/2 ins. in height, not counting high heels. I even tried kneeling on this occasion, but sleep eluded me in any pretzeled position.

Finally we arrived. The joy occasioned by the hot, wet blanket effect of the opened cabin door was only slightly dampened by the waiting, sweaty, crabby bank official who informed us that we were over a day late. As if we didn't know! I think he misread our foolish grins as a lack of sympathy for his inconvenience. We were so glad to be home.

Even though we were late back, the bank wasn't quite ready for us because the flat in which we would be living was still occupied by someone who hadn't yet gone on leave.

"Does this mean that we are staying in Lagos?" I asked, trying to walk with crossed fingers, toes and knees.

It did! It also meant that we'd be living in Ikoyi, not too far from the club! I had definitely died and gone to heaven this time!

For now a kind, senior bank official who had plenty of room in his house had offered to put us up. We didn't stay with him long but we enjoyed every minute of it. He lived next door to the compound of none other than Major-General Yakubu Gowon, Commander of the Armed Forces of Nigeria and in this military government, head honcho of the whole country. In such a location, many of the little inconveniences experienced by others simply do not exist. The electricity, for instance, went on and stayed on. During our visit there were no blackouts and no brownouts. The windows were devoid of *anti-t'ief* bars since would-be *t'ief-men* (thieves) preferred to ply their trade away from platoons of armed soldiers. There was one final advantage: our senior banking friend loved snails and he taught me.

Coming from a soggy climate like England where every cabbage-patch my Dad ever tended had more than its share of rotten things like slugs, snails and caterpillars, I had never seriously considered eating anything of that ilk. Eating the mangled cabbages was trial enough. However, the *Quo Vadis* restaurant, situated on the penthouse floor of the beautiful Western House building at the end of Lagos Marina boulevard, had more going for it than just the view. According to our host, it also had the best snails. When I finally gave in to the garlic-laden fumes wafting from the fork our new friend insisted on waving under my nose, I discovered that snails were indeed glorious. What's more, they weren't chewy. I'd always expected that they'd be chewy. So, we had snails for appetizer, snails for a main course, and snails for dessert. Move over, *fattouche!* By the time we had finished my first meal of snails, we had got outside of nine dozen, and the pile of shells in the center of the table resembled one of the groundnut pyramids in the Northern state. Unfortunately, I have never since found snails anywhere else that tasted as good as those at the *Quo Vadis.*

Shortly afterwards, we moved to the bank flats at the end of Ikoyi Island and I went back to the problem of interviewing stewards. Mamadu and Garubas I and II were remembered with much gusty sighing. Eventually we settled on Sunday, and he remained with us during most of my remaining days in paradise. Sunday was young, possibly in his early twenties, and his ambition was to one day be a driver. Meanwhile, he was a pretty fair steward, except when he had one of his aberrations. For instance, he made a great red snapper casserole. We ate it quite often. Nobody ever discovered why on one occasion he decided to use the whole fish: head, tail, scales, and for all we knew, innards. We just went back to the club and ate. On another occasion I had instructed him that we were bringing another master home for chop and Sunday served fish and baked beans-and nothing else. It could be argued that I should have given more thorough instructions, but I let my stewards serve what they wanted almost whenever they wanted, and that way I had had some excellent meals that I wouldn't otherwise have discovered they could cook. This is how we found out about Sunday's maple coconut pudding. What a fantastic dessert! I should never have left the country without getting his recipe.

Recipes tended to be a problem if you wanted a steward to follow one. Many stewards had only the most rudimentary schooling. When that fact was added to the limitations of pidgin English and several tribal dialects, there was the basis of some major food foul-ups. Soon after the red snapper casserole casualty, I thought to ask Sunday what was for dinner, before I went to the club.

"Is mombrake, madame," he told me.

"What's *mombrake?*" I inquired. He had on occasion surprised us with something unusual and very good, like that maple coconut pudding.

"Oh, is good, madame. Is eggs and cheese and ever't'ing, madame."

Our appetites were whetted to the point where we actually came home for dinner on time for once. Guess what? Mombrake is omelet. To think we could have had another couple of games of snooker! (At least it wasn't followed by celery and custard!)

Another area of confusion centered around shopping lists. It was best to have whoever was going shopping make out the list. That way Sunday knew he meant cucumber when he wrote *gogoman* and onions when he wrote *oinies*.

Meanwhile, the war wore on. The roadblocks were the most constant reminder. They were everywhere. Also, we had to carry our passports with us at all times to prove identity. Since I favored never changing my day-to-day handbag until it fell to pieces, my passport began to look quite disgusting with lipstick smears and splashes of Caladryl. (Caladryl was the best instant cure for the itch of mosquito-bites. Everyone carried it.)

Strangely enough, our handbags were rarely searched. On one of the few occasions mine was, the soldier pulled out item after item without comment and set them down on a makeshift wooden table by the roadblock. He finally came to my two precious Innoxa lipsticks. Innoxa was not a brand available in Nigeria, and these special extra-lanolin items had to either be brought from home or received in the mail with an import duty fee of 100% (rather like the import duty on musical instruments!)

The soldier took the top off one, shook it, turned it upside-down, and finding no obvious use for it, settled on its suspicious shape and demanded to know what I was doing hiding these bullets.

"What?" I screeched. "I'll have you know that these are lipsticks! Look'um!" and proceeded to paint over whatever color I was already wearing.

He waved me through. I don't know if he was convinced, but I think the fury he encountered when my last lipsticks were threatened put him off.

I didn't win them all, though. Another time I was on a long drive and had a thermos of coffee in the car. I had to stop at a roadblock, and there was no convincing the soldier in charge that my thermos was not a weapon. I even poured him some coffee. Too bad. He insisted on keeping thermos, coffee and all.

The most amusing thing that happened regarding road blocks was the edict whereby soldiers must search all boots. Literal to the end, they kept making us take our shoes off. Frequently in this confusion the trunk of the car never even got opened. We got into the habit of driving in our bare feet with our flip-flops held out of the window. It speeded up the road-block process quite a bit.

CHAPTER 16

After leave, as soon as I had spent a few days at the pool to rid myself of British Winter White-my husband used to say that all English people except the Cornish (naturally) soaked their legs in bleach every night-I looked around for a job. A call came in from one of the community's most prominent Syrian businessmen. He had received glowing reports of my work from my dear old Syrian importer in Jos, as well as from the two brothers at whose perfume factory I had worked on a temporary basis. With the call came an invitation to lunch for my husband and me.

I made a point of never refusing a Middle Eastern invitation to any meal. These people know good food when they see it! The house was as outstanding as the food, and we had a most enjoyable three hours. The visit was embellished by some time in their swimming pool, which was heart-shaped and extended into the waters of Five Cowrie Creek. A couple of hours had gone by before I realized that this was some kind of interview in itself. Were we the kind of people who would do credit to Syria's image in Africa? We must have passed muster; it was suggested I apply at the Embassy.

The Syrian Embassy in Lagos was at that time located six floors up in a skyscraper on Yakubu Gowon St., but thankfully relocated to a lovely villa on Alhaji Ribadu Road alongside Five Cowrie Creek a couple of weeks after I was hired. Six floors up is not far when the lifts work, but with Nigeria's erratic electricity I soon felt my thigh muscles beginning to develop. I also remember in particular one 45-minute imprisonment between floors in a lift with four local tradesmen. When the electricity goes out the lift stops and the air conditioning dies too. I remember that the tradesmen in question were not merely glowing like Rita Hayworth.

The villa, though, was a delightful place to work. Originally meant as a typical spacious expat abode, it had two floors of gleaming terrazzo and plenty of rooms to make offices for everyone. We made a lobby out of the large reception room inside the main doors, and the large, airy, high-ceilinged room beside it became the Ambassador's office. The rest of us took offices on the ground floor, except for the First Secretary. He was a distinguished-looking gray-haired man who liked to keep an open bottle of whisky in his bottom right desk drawer. He also liked to keep his shirt off in the office. Maybe the alcohol in his blood kept his temperature up. Anyway, he correctly worked out that if anyone was coming to see him he would hear their footsteps on the stairs and would have time to close the drawer and put on his shirt.

The Ambassador was a quiet, formal man who always treated me with the utmost politeness. His first request was that my daily greeting would be "*S'bagh el khaire.*" "Good morning," in Arabic. He was pleased that I had learned a certain amount of the language and encouraged me to continue. He had a ten year-old son, Bashir, who was the light of his life. Bashir was a mischievous kid who appealed to me greatly. His visits were enjoyed by all the staff, even the lugubrious Mr. Quadri, a cadaverous Ethiopian who spent most of his time hunched over an Arabic typewriter, muttering to himself.

Most of my work came via the Attache, who was the most fluent in English. I should say Texan, since that was where he had gone to college and his speech was peppered with *cotton-picking* this and that. He discovered I had no objections to attending to his personal correspondence as well as business. He would contract *cotton-picking* to *c.p.* and a few of those sprinkled throughout a letter made it sound as though he had written it himself. We became fast friends. He would even give me a ride to and from work in the mornings. The Embassy was open only in the morning, six days a week. The Attache drove a yellow Volkswagen with the heater vents stuck on. I was the only person he had met apart from himself who could stand to be in his car in darkest Africa, 200 miles from the equator, in temperatures of 90+ and humidity of up to 98 degrees-with the heater on!

Every month, each Embassy would disseminate information. This was blatant propaganda and took the form of two legal sized pages of mimeographed newsletter. When I took over, ours tended to be a bit tongue-in-cheek, but it should be understood that I was one of the neo-colonialist imperialists I was given to denounce. I also set up two trade missions. This impressed on me the power of diplomatic double talk, since I managed to arrange both events without having a very clear idea of what a trade mission was. All missives from one diplomatic mission to another, or to the Ministry of External Affairs, through which all official efforts were directed, had to be written in the third person. There were also certain phrases which must be incorporated into each letter, such as "presenting its compliments" and "assuring" whoever "of its highest consideration." Once you had strung together all the mandatory phrases, you only had to fill in a blank or two here and there and you could do anything from arrange a trade mission to (presumably) start a war.

I had a good time updating the files and speeding up the process of sending out propaganda by inaugurating mimeographed mailing labels. Heaven knows how they had ever managed to get the first one out before. Not that it mattered. I felt sure that our propaganda received from the other diplomatic missions the same attention we gave theirs. Zilch. The prettiest brochures were always arranged around a table in the lobby, though. I liked the reception room to look nice.

The staff of the Embassy was wonderful to me and gave me many of the privileges which were rightfully only those of diplomats. Whenever they ordered liquor at diplomatic rates, approximately six shillings or a dollar a bottle, they included an order for me. This did plenty for my popularity rating in a country where imported booze was severely restricted due to being in the middle of a civil war. At our dinner parties there was always plenty of Dewar's White Label before dinner, and Rose d'Anjou with it.

It was somewhere around this time that I met my great friend Kath. We were a lot alike in size, which was very handy on Saturday afternoons in the rains when we would take all the English size 36's and the American 7's into Leventis' department store ladies' changing rooms and both try on everything without having to venture back to the racks. We rarely bought anything. We were both handy with a needle, Kath had her own sewing machine, and in any case my tailor would run up copies of any item of clothing I gave him, for a nominal fee.

Kath was four years my junior and had the enviable history of being partially brought up on the Coast. Her dad was presently head of the CID in Lagos. Most of her Nigerian domicile had been in Sapele in the Mid-West, and much of this time her father had been on the hit list of a couple of prominent Nigerian politicians. He had spent a while hiding out in the jungle and used to creep by the house for food like a *t'iefman* in the night. I thought the whole thing was unbelievably romantic.

Kath's dad was half Flemish, half Belgian, and an accomplished linguist. At one point in his career he had been President De Gaulle's interpreter. His wife was a slight, dark-haired beauty of Indonesian descent who happened to be deaf and dumb. Kath, her elder sister and younger brother all signed with fluency. The family held British passports and had English accents despite the years prior to Nigeria, when they lived in many western European countries and at times spoke nothing but German, French or Spanish. Kath herself had a slightly exotic look. She had big, dark eyes and thick, wavy hair which became so unruly when long that she usually wore it in a short, glossy cap. She was as tall as me, and we would preen when a mutual friend addressed us as "You two long-stemmed lovelies."

While I spoiled the otherwise unsullied serenity of the Embassy in the mornings by caroling happily to myself as I skipped up and down the staircase, Kath was let loose in the hell that was the Montessori School. What's more, she liked it. I said that I liked the girl. I never said she wasn't crazy. In those days, before having kids of my own, I used to feel it would be a good idea if children were born at about age 20. Kath just loved them. All of them. Regardless of status of potty training.

Imagine a kindergarten in Lagos. Imagine over 30 children of almost 30 nationalities, all together for probably the first time away from Mum and the steward and the nanny, all speaking some sort of language but rarely the same as any other one of the kids, and all with different social values regarding hygiene. All the kids from any given town in England or the U.S. will have slightly imperfect rules of hygiene, but we are now talking about some kids who have never even *seen* a toilet, let alone have any idea what the thing is for. For some reason it is usually assumed to be a toy, and making things disappear by flushing is a great game. Making other kids disappear by flushing is frowned upon, so each visitor to the bathroom is accompanied by an adult, like Kath. She was explaining her job to me once and I discovered it included 32 trips to the bathroom in one morning session of school. (None of these trips was for Kath herself, of course.) When not in the bathroom, she spent a lot of time explaining to the children that they were supposed to sit down, preferably in one of the chairs provided. Many of the children were brought up in African homes where chairs may not have been available and discipline in the western sense did not exist. Other children might have been the offspring of Ambassadors of foreign cultures where it was customary to sit on the floor. And so on. And so on.

Our mutual friend, Molly, an Englishwoman who had two boys of her own and thought she liked kids, was persuaded to teach Montessori's kindergarten at the start of one term. I called her at work and couldn't hold a conversation due to what was obviously an air raid in progress at her end. When we met in the club that night, she downed a much-needed cocktail and announced that she had quit.

"After one morning?" I asked.

"No. Before the morning was over," she said. We shook our heads over Kath, who had calmly soldiered on through this chaos, and who had informed Molly that it was always like that.

"Of course," she had told Molly, "the first day is always the most confusing. They will learn to sit down in a week or two."

CHAPTER 17

West African wildlife was mostly to be found in nightclubs. The other variety was much scarcer: in five years I saw a column of ants, a bush cat, and a snake. The snake was at least sixty feet away. I did hear some elephants once, but it surprised me greatly that I although could hear elephants trumpeting in bush, I couldn't find them. You'd think that something the size of an elephant would be hard to hide, regardless of how many trees there were.

Now the nightclubs *were* wild. The rugby club members were particularly fond of the *Caprice*, located in the Hotel Domo and referred to simply as the *Domo*. My favorite was the *Bagatelle*, referred to as the *Baggers*. There was also a great nightclub at the Excelsior Hotel in Apapa, where I saw the best belly-dancing floor show ever. Two girls gyrated down the length of the table, clicking their little finger cymbals and never missing a beat. They did miss every glass and plate on the table. Not altogether unimpressive. *Le Paon Rouge* (the Red Peacock) had a good floor show on occasion, as did the Federal Palace Hotel.

It was usual on a Saturday night for a group of us to meet at someone's house for drinks at about 8 p.m., go to the *Domo* at 9:30 for dinner and dancing, then transfer to the *Baggers* at about 1:00 a.m. and dance until there was nobody else left; usually between 7:00 and 9:00 a.m. The music was all records, but they were always the top of the pops at the time, and included some banned items which the owners had brought in via Beirut. The dancing never stopped during the twelve hours or so that the clubs were open.

Dancing for several hours at a stretch in a crowded nightclub, albeit air-conditioned, would sweat away any extra pounds their excellent cuisine tried to add. My hair would become sodden seaweed down my back. One such evening, when the Ladies Room was out of order due to a flood from one of the commodes, I was sitting at the bar between dances, trying to get a comb through my hair. The man sitting on the next stool swiveled to face me and said, *"Sie kammte es mit goldenem kamme, Und sangt ein lieb dabei...."*

I couldn't let pass the only occasion I have ever been given to spout one of my favorite poems: *"Das hat eine wundersame, Gewaltlige melodei."* I chanted the last two lines triumphantly with him. Impressed. Definitely a new line in chat-up.

"The Lorelei," I said. He admitted he hadn't expected me to know it, and I didn't admit that those were the only four lines I did know. And I wasn't that sure how to spell them, either. The poem tells of the famous mermaid combing her hair with a golden comb and singing a haunting song. (Well, I can't sing....)

Since the newcomer had had a book of poetry published in his youth it was not surprising that he knew a wide variety of other poems too. He turned out to be an executive of my husband's bank, who was visiting from London. I like to remember him as being representative of some of the interesting people who kept turning up on the Coast.

However, our friend Keith must be credited with one of the best chat-up lines of all time. He was seated at a bar one night when a very attractive female, whom he did not recognize, sat on the next stool.

"Hello," he said. "I'm usually not as tall as this but I'm sitting on my wallet."

They began chatting. After a few drinks she began telling him her life story. It wasn't very happy and she started to cry. Keith handed her his handkerchief. She dried her tears and handed it back. Suddenly, Keith screamed, threw the hanky away, and fell backwards off his chair.

"There's a centipede in it!" he yelped. The barman gingerly picked up the offending piece of cloth and shook it. Out fell half a set of false eyelashes!

One way to get the attention of women is to own a pet which is special or unusual. There was the regular complement of dogs and cats on the Coast, and also a large number of parrots. The West African Gray is an expensive and not very colorful parrot, but its high cost reflects its superior ability to talk.

A young banking friend named Allan bought himself a West African Gray. Since he was with Standard Bank, and Barclays Bank DCO was their main competitor, the first words he taught his new pet were, "Bugger Barclays! Bugger Barclays!"

Allan drank too much and smoked too much. This was brought home to him when the parrot regaled a group of his friends with a perfect rendition of its master's morning hacking and coughing, ending with an exhausted, "Kee-rist!!" The parrot also let all his friends know what he said the morning he awoke late, hung over, and bruised, to find his car bumper laid carefully across his bedside table.

Meanwhile, we got another cat. This one was unnervingly like Snowy both in looks and attitude; again, half Siamese and half tabby. Its eyes were unwinking blue and its fur was cream touched with coffee. Its brain was psychotic touched with manic depressive. We called it *Buggsy* after Buggsy Siegel, because he was such a criminal. This was before we found out he was a she.

Buggsy liked me and she liked my husband. She tolerated Sunday because he gave her food. I think he was afraid not to. She disliked my Platters records and took neat little V-shaped bites out of them. Luckily, Elvis escaped her disapproval. She hated anyone to come to dinner in a silk tie and would fix those ties with her claws so that they were never fit for knotting again. She also knew, the way cats do, who didn't like cats. Our friend Keith, for one. So she would always single him out for special attention. Usually she would plaster herself beside the skirting board so that she wasn't obtrusive, and slide around the perimeter of the room until she was behind Keith's chair. Without warning, she would leap over his shoulder and attempt to get a good grip on his chest with all her claws. She needed a good grip because Keith would leap out of his chair with a screech, splash beer all over and hit his head on the fan. In the ensuing melee a cat could get hurt if she wasn't properly dug in.

Everybody always enjoyed this little cabaret. Except Keith. However, Sunday made pretty good curry so he kept coming back.

Buggsy also like curry. In fact, she loved it and would give Sunday no peace until he gave her some. She always got fed before us. The night after a curry we would have the leftovers as curry casserole, and the third night whatever remained was blended into curry soup. We were therefore reduced to fighting our pet for food. Sunday was more scared of her than of us, so curry didn't often last till the third night, regardless how much Sunday had originally made. As long as it smelled like curry, Buggsy wanted her share. We had so much in common. Her other favorite dish was rice pudding.

Buggsy had the run of the flat and showed no interest in going downstairs to the great outdoors. Except twice. She got pregnant both times. I was impressed when I saw her pee directly into the plug hole of the bathroom sink. Now I wonder why I didn't try to train her to use the toilet if she was so smart she could work out the sink bit all by herself.

We worried about her the first time she went downstairs and stayed out all night, and our worst fears were realized when she started to get pumpkin-shaped.

She used to sleep at the top of the bed in the tent made by my long hair falling over the back of the pillow. I had tried to discourage her coming into the bedroom when she was a kitten but she had mewed so piteously that I had relented. It was all a ploy. She was always mean enough to take what she wanted. However, she learned not to massage my scalp with her claws while she purred, so she stayed.

One night I was awakened by a squeaking sound. It came from behind my pillow. Buggsy was having kittens under my hair! Two were born already, little white rats with bleary eyes; and it looked as though there were more where that came from. I felt strongly that under my hair was not a good idea but I hadn't considered an alternative maternity site. Picking up Buggsy and offspring in two anxious batches, I deposited them in the bath. Buggs appeared to be happy enough there and continued to clean off the bugglets. I went back to bed. By morning there were two more like the first two, and although Buggsy's personality never became totally congenial, she did show some signs of maternal affection. Somehow we never got around to giving away any of Buggsy's brood. They were all pretty and obviously part-Siamese, and Sunday appeared more at home with them than he ever did with their mother.

One year later, she did it again! This time Buggsy betook herself to the bath first, and had all four kittens there. The new four looked like the old four, and suddenly there were nine cats all over the flat.

CHAPTER 18

Life at the Syrian Embassy was never boring. My diplomats treated me like a queen and introduced me with pride to the parade of visiting ambassadors who dropped by on courtesy calls and invited my diplomats to a constant round of receptions and parties. My favorite was the Hungarian Ambassador. He was a rotund, bouncing little man who charmed everyone with whom he came into contact, and never held it against me when I ran him down with my surfboard one Sunday at Lighthouse Beach.

Some of the visiting diplomats would ask if I could recommend secretaries for their embassies, and I garnered an undeserved reputation as provider of exceptional secretarial talent when I mentioned to the Iraqi Ambassador that the new bride of one of our banking friends, a bright and attractive Irish girl, was thinking of getting a job. She was great and he was fulsomely grateful, in true Arabic fashion. For this signal favor the moon would not have been too much for me to ask. Years later in Beirut he took me out to dinner several times, still giving thanks for my recommendation.

Nobody even thought to chastise me when I reversed my sporty little Fiat into the Embassy flagpole, leaving identical dents in both my bumper and the white painted pole. As long as Madame was not hurt....

Our Embassy's turn came to host a reception. Although it was not usual practice to include any staff other than the diplomats attached to the Embassy in question, my diplomats invited my husband and me and included any friends I might care to bring. Naturally I asked Kath, and she brought Derek, her boyfriend of the moment. This almost led to an international incident.

I was sipping my cocktail and behaving when the Indian Ambassador sidled up with the suggestion, "I am thinking it will be very nice if we are having dinner together. You can be coming to my house after this is over."

I wriggled out of this invitation with a smile and an explanation to do with my husband and I having already made plans. Undaunted, he turned to Kath with the suggestion that they see a movie.

"What did you say?" demanded her boyfriend, three gin-tonics aggressive.

"I am explaining this young lady something that is not your business," retorted Don Juan of Calcutta. His high and mighty attitude invoked the less-than-respectful response, "The lady is with me. Keep your paws to yourself!"

The conversation had reached the "Do you know who I am?" stage by the time Kath, my husband and I dragged her beau backwards into the bushes and smoothed some ruffled diplomatic feathers. It was a worrying moment for me. I would never have forgiven myself for being even remotely part of a fracas. It would have reflected very badly on people who had gone out of their way for me so consistently. It *was* the last time I attended a diplomatic reception. (Unless you count the times we gate-crashed the American Embassy barbeques.) However, that was different. We used to do that because it was one of the few places to get barbequed ribs in Lagos, and these strange American men never employed stewards to cook out, but would stand at the grill themselves for hours, passing out hundreds of pounds of ribs to anyone passing a hopeful plate. They enjoyed it, so we considered it a service.

My diplomats also used to let me leave the office for an hour or so on the occasions of their wives' *kaffee klatches,* as soon as my passion for

Arabic food became evident. I used to smuggle back a couple of those little individual pizzas flavored with cinnamon and oregano for Muyinot, the Nigerian Embassy receptionist. Muyinot was a pretty girl who would click the back of her chair on the wall to warn me if the Ambassador was walking purposefully towards my office on any of the days when I had not had time to go to bed the previous night. Social life in Lagos was serious stuff, and frequently something had to go to accommodate all that there was to do. Usually it was sleep. Provided that work was up to date I had been known to get forty winks with my head on my arms, using the typewriter as a pillow.

Hell on the Coast. Right?

The rains came and so did the litter from the other Embassies and the Ministry of Information. One statistic wasn't lost amid all that paper. We had 42 inches of rain in July, 1968. The place started to look as though Noah was due any day. Eighteen inches of water gurgled across Kakawa Street behind the bank, and on the days I drove my husband to work in our old Volkswagen, we had a bow wave like a Chriscraft. Nobody's brakes worked, so everyone just stopped by the simple expedient of flowing gently into the back of the vehicle in front. Volkswagens seemed to have an advantage due to their excellent under-sealing and those sensible bumpers which at the time were sufficiently far from the car body not to bend body-work in cases of over-enthusiastic stopping.

The gardens at the rear of the Embassy turned into a four-inch deep lake. Then, as the flowers fell from the Flame of the Forest tree, they lay on the water like an undulating red carpet. Even in a flood the place was beautiful.

A acquaintance had invited his girlfriend out to visit him for the summer. I would have felt sorry for her, not being able to enjoy the beaches, the boating, the sports and the vistas which were all such a part of our usual routine, except for the fact of her being another female in paradise.

Small world-she turned out to be an old classmate of my younger brother's. That was about as much introductory chat as we could manage, what with the offers of dinners, dancing and other entertainment showered upon her as a new single woman in that surfeit of single men. She spent much of her visit in the Ikoyi Club bar, as did we in the rains. And she was no more bored than we ever were.

Our little gang of mostly English expats also made a new friend at that time. We got to know the congenial American Operations Manager of Texaco's marketing division, and he would join us after work for our regular few hours of snooker and drinks. Banking had for so long been the subject of conversation that oil companies made a pleasant change. It appeared that Texaco was looking for a secretary for its Managing Director. Our new friend Bill suggested that I apply. I didn't jump at it. After all, I was very happy at the Embassy and I did get afternoons at the pool. However, he was very persuasive and eventually I checked it out. The result was an offer I couldn't refuse.

My diplomats were characteristically sweet but worried. If my leaving were a matter of money, then such-&-such a businessman could employ me for so many hours on two afternoons a week, and I could work for another one for so many hours the other afternoons, etc. etc. I hardened my heart and left, but promised to drop in and visit once in a while.

Next to going to the Coast in the first place, the best thing I ever did was to work for Texaco. My new boss was wonderful. A hail-fellow-well-met New Englander with a ruddy face and orange hair, he referred to himself as *MOM*. This was short for *Mean Old Man* and could not have been farther from the truth. People would say, "Oh, you're *his* secretary? Lucky you!" They were right. He was a hard worker who never let all night parties or *WAWA*-type Ministry negotiations interfere with his cheerful demeanor and the completion of Texaco's required paperwork.

There was still a war on. The east was still closed. Most of the oil at that time was in the east so the necessity to market it was severely curtailed.

"Take Tuesday afternoons off and go shopping," suggested my new boss. "When the east opens up there'll be plenty of work for us all to catch up on." Of course, I managed to get my grocery shopping done in another lunch hour so that it didn't interfere with this gratuitous gift of pool-time.

Grocery shopping in Lagos was a real treat for me after Jos and Benin. As well as good old Kingsway, there were several other stores, in particular one Lebanese and one Indian, where a fine selection of groceries was displayed for sale. A good customer might also get some goods which were not necessarily always on display. I really liked Nassar's Lebanese supermarket. They would make a superb, garlicky *hummus* fresh for a dinner party, and they never let me go without Lee & Perrin's Worcester sauce, even in the thick of the war. Many day-to-day items were hard to find as imports got more and more restricted. Most stewards learned to make ketchup from scratch, and a couple of recipes for home-made mayonnaise made the rounds constantly. I never bothered with either. As long as Nigeria didn't run out of its glorious, explosive, red pepper and those vicious little green peppers which looked for all the world like baby green bell peppers! However, there is no substitute for Lee & Perrin's. Standing in the store looking lost would inevitably attract the attention of one of the store owners, who would always produce from the back whatever item or condiment I had been unable to locate anywhere else in Lagos.

When grocery shopping in Nigeria was concluded, madame would lead the way to the car, followed by four or five little African boys, each balancing a full cardboard box of groceries on his head. A small dash to each and they would skip off, grinning, to be of service to the next shopper.

Consider how civilized this whole business is. Every time one of us came back from leave we would have stories of the miseries of shopping U.K.-style. Kath earned my sympathy over grocery shopping on leave in Wednesbury. "I forgot you have to carry all those bags to the supermarket," she said, "and I was just standing there when the checkout lady snapped at me for not packing my own stuff. Then everybody else got mad because I

had nothing to put it in. Then I couldn't get it to the car because I had had
to park it miles away. The whole thing was so embarrasing."

There was also the problem of the overpriced cabbage. On the Coast
we got most of our vegetables from the market. Maybe the steward would
go, or maybe madame would go. Either way it was usual to bargain. At
least we had a chance of paying what we thought was a reasonable price
for any particular item. In England on leave, one friend forgot her whereabouts for a moment:

"How much is this cabbage?" she asked.

"One and sixpence, madam," replied the sales assistant.

"I'll give you ninepence for it," said Valerie.

"But madam," the clerk was shocked. "It's one and six!"

One day in Nassar's supermarket, I overheard an American priest complaining because the war import restrictions meant that he could only get
smooth peanut butter, and not his favorite crunchy style. Coming from
consumer heaven (America-where a dozen ready-made selections grace
the shelves of even the smallest grocery store) it had not occurred to him
that he was living in the peanut capital of the world. Only a few years
previously, before independence, Nigeria had maintained its balance of
payments with its groundnut crop. A request to any half-decent steward
would have fixed his problem.

As I mentioned previously, other necessities also came to a screeching
halt. While I worked for the Embassy the lack of imported alcohol was no
problem, but afterwards like everyone else I had to resort to a smuggler.
The Nigerian smuggler at that time was an entrepreneur with a class act.
He would sidle into banks, oil companies, and other expat institutions
armed with an order book. After writing down everyone's order he'd leave,
and would return anything from an hour to a week later clanking suspi-
ciously in his native robes. Out of this baggy trouser pocket would come
a bottle of scotch; from another a bottle of brandy. Out of the folds of his
agbada would appear a London gin. His prices were fair and a lot less than

we paid when imports again began to trickle in. Besides, it gave us a kick to refer to *our smuggler* as offhandedly as one would normally refer to *our accountant* or *our lawyer.*

CHAPTER 19

It's a small world. I come from a small town named St. Austell, situated near the south coast of Cornwall in England's west country. Out of the dozen or so expatriates in Texaco's marketing division there happened to be a Sales Manager who also hailed from St. Austell. (The Cornish who live there refer to it as *Snausel.*) Cornwall has a very long history of tin-mining dating back to at least the time of the Phoenicians. It is also the location of the famous Camborne School of Mines. This means that Cornishmen are to be found all over the world wherever there are mines. It is jokingly said that every Cornishman has a Cousin Jack somewhere for whom he is incessantly trying to get a job. The Cornish are therefore always being referred to as *Cousin Jacks*. George Hooper found it hard to believe that another Cousin Jack (albeit female) from so close to his home had fetched up only two doors down from his office in Africa. He popped in to check out my bona fides.

"'Ello. From Snausel be 'ee 'en?" (Translation, "Hello. From St. Austell are you, then?")

I grinned and drew breath in sharply between pursed lips. In Cornwall this means *Yes*. To the uninitiated, it sounds as though you have just hurt yourself slightly-maybe pricked a finger or something.

We had a conversation mostly in the vernacular, which totally mystified my new boss and the other sales people watching, both the English and American. We couldn't pass up any opportunity to further confuse everyone; and from that day on he would say good morning by banging open my office door and yelling something like, "Shut yer bleddy mouth, maid!" and then disappearing in the direction of his own office.

"What did he say?" was the onlookers' usual query.

"Shut your bloody mouth, girl," I would explain. They usually shook their heads; but it made some kind of Cornish sense to me.

George was an Old Coaster of many years' standing. His wife, Inez, had not forgotten how to make the best pasties in that hemisphere. A pasty (pronounced *pah-stee* for benefit of those Americans I am still trying to educate!) is the result of the Cornish history of tin-mining. The poor tinners used to disappear down the mines for long, dark days, and their canny spouses had invented a kind of hemispherical pastry-covered meat, potato, onion and turnip pie which would retain heat over a long period. At least the tinners of old ate a hot mid-day meal, even when they had gone down the pit before daylight. It was always a treat when Inez was in the mood to hunt down some scented yellow turnips from the markets. She'd make a batch of fresh pasties and we would all gather together and pig out, while the accents degenerated more and more into the Cornish-*er* and-*ar* vernacular. (Americans, think Long John Silver.)

George and Inez were typical expats, always game for a party. Our boss had a great patio with a bar at one end, the whole area overhung by a glorious Flame of the Forest tree. Many happy evenings were spent at the bar, caroling *My Heart Cries for You* to an old Guy Mitchell record, every beat punctuated with a slosh of George's brandy and my gin-tonic.

My boss's initials were J.O.S. Texaco always used initials to identify mail routing, and it followed that the executives themselves would be referred to by their initials. It was hard luck that J.O.S. spelled Jos, and so of course all mail addressed to John O. Sheldon would be routed the thousand miles to Jos on the plateau before being re-routed back to Lagos, with a note to the mailroom clerks to take it down their own corridor. It was all part of life's rich pattern. The real problem was the time this took. Weeks, sometimes. A cable to the U.S. or U.K. took two hours. One to the plateau from Lagos took five days, more or less.

Letters to the U.K. usually only took about five days. I have always been an enthusiastic correspondent since I have a need to communicate which is not stifled by lack of an audience, either face-to-face or on a telephone. Our telephone system was able to connect calls to the U.K.; however, it wasn't really up to it on a constant and reliable basis. Part of the problem might have been the fact that when lifting the receiver one would often find oneself listening to a radio program. No amount of jiggling the hook would interfere with this. It was merely necessary to go away and try again later. So, when all else failed I would write letters. Our technicolor daily life was so different from the black and white reality of England that I *had* to tell somebody. One who read and wrote back regularly was my best friend, Pauline Brown.

Paul and I were the same age and had come to work at a bank in St. Austell when we were 16, within three months of one another. We were something of a Mutt and Jeff partnership: I was noticeably tall and she was noticeably not; also she was curvy enough that our fellow bank clerks had nicknamed her *Busty Brown*. To put it kindly, I was aerodynamic. We had become friends and spent a great deal of time together. Most of that time we giggled. It never had to be at anything particular. She happened to have the world's most infectious giggle and it would start me off, too.

I had spent a lot of ink trying to persuade Paul to join me in paradise. The day came when she had broken off an engagement and had no further immediate need to save her pennies.

"Come and visit!" I had pleaded.

"Dammit, I will!" her letter replied.

This news was received with rejoicing not only by me, but by all the woman-hungry masculinity at the club. They promptly began staking their claims by playing poker for her, making her the prize for numerous games of snooker and darts, and in general working out a roster of activities that would have the poor girl hospitalized with exhaustion in under a week. Friend Bill was one of those who never won any of those games; but you know what they say: "Lucky at cards, unlucky in love." Obviously the opposite also holds true. He happened to be the only guy who didn't have to work on the Saturday morning that Paul's plane touched down at Lagos' Ikeja airport. Noble and self-sacrificing as he was, he offered to drive me out to pick her up. The other males didn't have a chance. By the time we had returned to our flat he had secured dates for that night, the next night, and the foreseeable future. The grumbling heard around the club was dark and menacing but Bill smiled beatifically through it all and continued to have a wonderful time.

Texaco had a boat called the *Texaco Star*. (Not exactly unexpected, name-wise.) It had a 440 Volvo inboard engine and held an indeterminate number of people, since that number was defined solely by however many people wanted to go over to the beach at any one time. That's how many it held. There was a wooden roof over the cockpit about six feet in length. Never ones to let the grass grow under our feet or mix our metaphors where sun-tanning was concerned, Kath and I had discovered this to be a great place to lie full-length and get a start on our tan en route across the harbor. The Saturday morning when our little gang of some dozen or so individuals had decided to take Paul over to the beach for the weekend, Kath and I were prone on our customary tanning roof when the boat gauges went into the red zone. Overload! The driver deemed it necessary to stop....now! Kath and I sailed gracefully forward across the roof and over the bow of the boat in perfect parabolas. We surfaced spluttering, to be dragged back aboard by a group of young men who were quite overcome with hysterics. (It would have served them right if I'd made them take a banana boat next time!)

The major expat corporations on the Coast owned bungalows in the shade of the drooping casuarina trees at the back of the beach, for use by their staff on weekends and holidays. All that was necessary was to put one's name down to reserve the house, and then remember to take bed linens and mosquito nets as well as provisions. The bank bungalow was a typical beach structure, and like the *Texaco Star* it held as many persons as we felt inclined to invite. There were two bedrooms with two twin beds apiece. Separating the bedrooms was a long kitchen, open at both ends. One end led to an outside shower and toilet, the other to the porch. The porch was a roofed area with a floor, a large table, dining chairs and a several easy chairs flanked by the ubiquitous little drinks tables.

Unloading the provisions, particularly the Star beer, from the boat was a job needing the assistance of several of the small boys who hung around the dock looking for such dash-able tasks. There was a steward attached to each beach house, but he was more in the nature of a caretaker than a fully fledged steward, and this was where we might get the dubious pleasure of doing the cooking ourselves. Casseroles were therefore favorite fare. We'd get our own steward to make up a couple at home and then pop them in the gas oven ourselves once at the beach. Champagne, garlic bread and baked beans also appeared to be *de rigueur;* at least, they always turned up for breakfast on these weekends. I defy anyone who hasn't had champagne, baked beans and garlic bread for breakfast on a beach, after a night without a wink of sleep, to tell me it doesn't hit the spot.

We usually intended to sleep. Sort of. But after the usual rowdyism which attended any of our get-togethers, and a few outings to see what mischief we could wreak along the shore, and the fact that we had either forgotten the mosquito nets or their holes were larger than the mosquitoes, all hope of sleep would be banished and we would revert to the usual Sunday naps in the sunshine all day.

Swimming at night, however, was a fascinating experience in that bath-warm water. There was such phosphorescence that we would take turns leaping out of the water and guessing whose ghostly outline remained imprinted on our retinas for the split second before the phosphorescence winked out. Trailing hands in the water resulted in sparkling trails like comets. It was magical.

One night, as a diversion, it occurred to a few of us to see if we could move one of the palm-thatched huts from which sodas were dispensed during the daylight hours. Just as we had it lifted comfortably, we were assailed by the outraged cries of a night watchman. We hadn't thought about there being a night watchman on the beach. That was a stupid oversight. In Nigeria, anything needed a nightwatch if it wasn't nailed down.

"Make you go put um back one-time!" he bellowed.

"Oh shut up, you bloody idiot!" remarked by husband, the worse for a few beers.

"I not plotty idjot! You plotty idjot!" screamed the insulted native, running towards us across the sand. We saw that he was brandishing a machete. Discretion *is* the better part of valor. We scattered and ran. Ten minutes later as we hid in the long grass at the back of the beach, the man passed by two of us, still muttering to himself.

That's the only time I can remember taking my life in my hands at the beach, although occasionally we did surf in some seriously turbulent water.

There was also the problem of the over-friendly Military Governor with the Sandhurst accent, whose beach house was at the back of Lighthouse Beach, and who always insisted on playing his record of *The Girl from Ipanema* when I passed. That was a threat of a different nature, however.

A walk on Lighthouse Beach in the night was an interesting experience. Kath and I took a flashlight and went exploring in the early hours of one weekend morning. Trying to find our way by starlight and conserve batteries, we had strolled out into the middle of the beach.

"Listen!" she whispered, "Do you hear that?" A noise like the crackling of little dry pieces of paper completely surrounded us. It rustled, drew closer, and something scrabbled at my foot. I screamed, and Kath flicked the switch on her flashlight. Then she screamed. Millions of little red eyes looked back at us for a split second, then they scattered, rustling away left and right across the sand and burrowing under the ground or disappearing into the waves. Crabs! Zillions of crabs. There hadn't been a free foot of beach. The most pragmatic soul can be xenophobic when alone at night with the unexpected. Do crabs attack if not provoked? The pinch of even a small one hurts. What if we had sat down? What if we had left the light behind? It *was* the light which scared them off…

Back at the beach house the whole episode was quite amusing. Funny, in fact. Several others got up to investigate, taking the entire collection of flashlights with them. Those remaining were too deep into their beer and rugby songs to care.

"Here's to Heineken! Here's to Heineken!

I can never get enough (Get enough!) Heine-ke-en i-is love-ly stuff!"

The following Saturday at the beach we were approached by a fellow banker who was the beach house's resident for that weekend.

"I hear you had a good time last week," he said. "Our steward and some of his friends said that you kept up the whole neighborhood last Saturday night, and they wanted to know if we were planning to party the same way, in which case, they would go and spend the night on the mainland!"

CHAPTER 20

One of Texaco's Assistant Managers was transferred to Australia. The Assistant Managers' (we had had two, originally) expat secretary had gone on leave. In one of those typical small-world episodes which continually crop up in expatriate existence, the new secretary was my old friend Carole from Jos, whose job I had filled for a short time when she was on leave. Her husband, Ian, had recently been transferred by the bank to Lagos. She was a good secretary, and I enjoyed working with her.

The war continued. By this time the Federal troops were making inroads into the eastern states. The world was full of starving Biafran P/R misinformation and jokes. We heard a great deal about the tons of donated foodstuffs rotting on the docks in rebel-held territory. The usual stories about soldiers taking what they needed and selling the rest on the black market or leaving it to spoil were brought back by those adventurous souls who undertook journeys down to the east to check things out on behalf of their companies. On occasion, persons who had been living for the past few months in the east would turn up in Lagos. They all looked well-enough fed to us.

We were somewhat incensed by a scene we witnessed some lunch times, but probably as much because wine was an import forbidden to the rest of us as because of any empathy with those starving Biafrans. The Red Cross was in high profile in Lagos due to food stocks being transferred to the eastern states. Dr. August Lindt, head of the organization, used to take his lunch at *Antoine's*. This was the best restaurant in Lagos, run by our likable Lebanese friend Chakeeb, nicknamed *Shakey*. His was some of the best cuisine in the city, and included Indonesian *satays* and his own heavenly version of *canneloni*, and a celestial fish in white sauce entitled *Sole Normale*. While chatting to Shakey at the bar during lunch, we would watch Dr. Lindt make his entrance, followed by a minion cradling Dr. L's personal bottle of wine from his private stock. It's safe to assume that if he'd offered us a glass, our self-righteousness over the man's unwillingness to live closer to the level of those he was meant to help would have probably dissolved. Sometimes I really missed those embassy perks!

The stocks of Star beer and Heineken never ran out, though. This was in spite of Lagos having a Rugby Club which labored constantly to keep the levels down. They partied continually, once in a while interrupting their carousal long enough to play a game, break a few bones and spit out a tooth or two. The lack of teeth never interfered with either the drinking (deadens the nerves?) or the singing (deadens the ears!) At almost any hour, particularly the dark ones, quaint African rugby songs could be heard issuing from the bar:

"My girl's from Warri
Ever so sorry!
She's got a face like
The back end of a mammy lorry!
(Chorus) And in my future life
She's gonna be my wife.
How the hell do you know that?
She told me so!

My girl's from Kafanchan,
She doesn't need a man.

She doesn't give a damn
Because she is a les-bi-an!
(Chorus)

My girl's from Yashi,
She savvy bashi,
But she no bashi
Unless you give her dashi!"

And so on. Local color. Actually they didn't play rugby all year; in summer they played cricket. They drank and sang all year, though.

The Lagos Rugby Club tie was dark blue, dotted with small logos depicting the rear end of an elephant. They even had a song about the hole in the elephant's bottom. There was some story to the effect that the clubs in Kaduna and Lagos had tossed for the head or the tail, and Lagos had lost the toss. We nevertheless felt that we had got the best end of the deal-as it were.

The joy of expat living meant that you never actually had to grow up. Where the daily grind in the old country included being the 24-hour a day maintenance man for your house or flat, these tasks were completed by persons authorized by your company, or by the steward, driver, gardener or nightwatch. For a man it left plenty of time to get good at snooker, golf, darts, squash, elbow-bending or singing rugby songs. Women were freed of the drudgery of housework and cooking, and we got good at some of the above too. We also had uninterrupted tans and blue-painted toenails. The nails could be painted daily to coordinate with the outfit of the moment. Somehow I have never found time for this in other lives. Parties were rife and party-giving was a breeze.

"Sunday, we are having twenty people for dinner tomorrow night."

"Yes, madame." My bit done!

Sometimes the steward would be unable to obtain enough help in the kitchen on a party night to keep up the schedule and so madame might help out. On one memorable occasion we were to have a West African curry and the many side dishes weren't ready. I decided to help chop those vicious little green peppers which can knock your socks off and blow a hole in the top of your head simultaneously. The heat in the fan-less kitchen caused sweat to pour down my face. Putting down the knife, I used both hands to wipe off my dripping visage. Oh, the pain! Juice from the peppers burned the skin around both eyes and alongside my nose and mouth. The welts remained for several hours and the stinging didn't go away until the next day. Poor Sunday was left to make the best time he could alone.

One of the best things about showing off a foreign lifestyle to a friend, is the way you relive the wonder of it all through new eyes, and gain renewed amusement engendered by a fresh viewpoint. With Paul staying, we were reduced to jelly-legs with mirth the day we watched a steward pass by carrying his closed umbrella on his head, the curved handle partially obscuring his vision. Usually the African ability to carry anything on the head and retain perfect balance without noticeable effort was one I admired. I never saw a load dropped or broken. Retelling our tale later at the boss's patio bar brought forth his own experiences years before in a posting to Haiti. His family and another family nearby used to be great friends and would communicate by handwritten notes when the phone was not working, which was often. Their stewards would carry the notes. The stewards' hands and pockets might be free but because it came naturally to carry things on their heads, they would also carry the notes this way. There was a problem with this. The notes would frequently blow away. A rock to hold down the note was found to be the answer. Thereafter, whenever other expats saw a steward running by with a rock on his head, they correctly assumed that the Sheldons and the Hills were passing notes again.

After too few weeks of the usual round of club, beach, and parties, Paul and her growing collection of West African leather-work and thorn carvings had to return to the U.K. and the serious business of making a living. Bill was not going to be the only one to miss her.

Shortly thereafter, the Nigerian Premier, General Gowon, decided to get married. Another excuse for parties and celebration. Then Bill and Paul decided to get married. An excuse for positive hysteria! At least on my part. The date was set for July 6th and in thanks for their introduction, Bill offered to take me back to U.K. for the wedding. I now had an excuse for two of my regular occupations: a) trying on everything in Leventis', and b) having my tailor copy various items of clothing to go with the Leventis' loot. I finally settled on a large black hat (after purchasing at least two others in pink) and a dress and coat in pink which I had the tailor make in the style of the yellow outfit I had worn on my first journey to Africa. This is notably the closest I have ever come to sentiment.

I also kept my tailor busy making trouser suits in Dacron, liberally decorated with Nigerian embroidery. This is quite an art form and was at that time much in demand. I thought they'd like it in England. Friend Molly, who was about my height, asked if I'd like to buy one she had ordered from her tailor. Her husband objected to the amount of embroidery on the jacket.

"You look like the Federal Palace doorman," he complained.

While trying it on in her bedroom, I could hear a scuffle outside the door. The legs were too short, so I reluctantly abandoned the outfit and emerged to find Molly's husband holding their four-year old son Andrew by the ear.

"Now apologize!" ordered his dad.

"I'm sorry I was looking through the keyhole!" squealed the kid, and made his escape too fast to see his father break down into knee-slapping glee.

"That's my boy!" he guffawed.

Before Bill & Pauline's wedding date approached, the entire Texaco office contracted a foul summer cold. I swore that it was Doris' fault, as she had the first one. She was the receptionist who handled the switchboard. In spite of all requests and directives to the contrary she insisted on pronouncing Texaco *TezzAHco*. That even sounds like a sneeze! Doris used to amuse me with her array of hairstyles. Dividing off the hair into sections bound tightly into spikes by diamond thread was common, and some of these styles were very attractive when the spikes were woven into little crowns. Doris, however, liked the ones which looked as though a spider sat atop her head. She was particularly fond of having one six inch spike of bound hair aimed directly down in front of her nose like a take-off of a Norman helmet. I never understood why she wasn't cross-eyed after a day of that.

Nigeria was the only country in the world where it was necessary to have up-to-date health documents to get out as well as to get in. When I first left for the Coast, I had had to have shots for yellow fever, typhoid, cholera, smallpox, tetanus and T.B., among others. They all had different renewal dates; some six months, some three years, some seven. At the airport I got stopped because my smallpox shot was out of date. Minor panic, until they said they'd give me one right there at the airport. Major panic? The syringe was not new and resided in some milky fluid on a grubby desk. Presumably it was the right vaccine. There's no way to tell with me; smallpox shots have no effect whatsoever. Anyway, I wasn't about to miss my best friend's wedding, and her fiance had paid for my ticket, so I stuck out my arm and was duly jabbed, signed off and free to go.

There is a seven hour flight from Lagos to Heathrow, with stops at one city or more out of Kano: either Rome or Frankfurt. Bill and I were sitting, minding our business, during the flight when I let out a scream which brought the stewardess flying down the aisle. It felt as though someone had stuck a pick-axe low into the center of my forehead. This was my first experience of clogged sinuses on a descending flight. Luckily Bill was better prepared for his cold than I was and lent me a nasal spray and some pain-killers.

Next we had some hold-up in Rome, but we did reach Heathrow in time to meet Pauline, coming home from her London job for the same reason we had crossed the Pond. Getting to Heathrow is only half the journey to Cornwall. Next we caught a bus to Reading station, then the overnight train to the west country.

"Knock us up in plenty of time for St. Austell," we asked the conductor. He gave us only fifteen minutes' notice, and we eventually hustled poor Bill off the train in his shirt sleeves, half-washed. His first sight of his beloved's hometown was through travel-bleary eyes, the remains of a cold, and a day's worth of beard that he had had no time to shave off. (Anybody who knows St. Austell will attest it looks pretty much the same regardless.)

We had a good time on our short vacation. We drank asti spumante, our preferred champagne. We visited each other's relatives. We ate half a dozen of Mum's pasties and guzzled whole pound trays of Cornish cream with fresh strawberries. We told stories about the civil war.

The wedding was lovely. Paul looked gorgeous in white velvet, diminutive next to 6 ft. Bill. The natives milled around him getting him to talk so that they could try to understand his accent. He gave up on theirs, even allowing for previous practice with George Hooper and me.

Paul's brother stood in for the best man, a friend from Lagos who was home on leave and had had the bad timing to come down with malaria while visiting his parents in London. We went to see him en route back. Malaria is frequently recurrent, though years can go by between attacks. Usually the reason for contracting it in the first place is simply not to take the prophylactic pills given freely to their staff members by the expat corporations. Whatever the reason he caught the disease, we had to feel sorry for our friend. His temperature was 105 degrees in spite of the blankets piled on the bed because he felt so cold. He had been delirious during the previous night. From where we sat across the room, we could see the entire bed shake with his tremors. By the time he recovered he had lost fifteen pounds, but by then we were back on the Coast.

Paul moved into Bill's Lagos apartment and completed his tour with him, then they finally had their delayed honeymoon in Europe. Afterwards they were transferred to New York. They never came back to the Coast.

CHAPTER 21

On July 20, 1969, Neil Armstrong walked on the moon. Shortly there-after, Lagos was the location of an outbreak of acute conjunctivitis. This was a new disease to the average Nigerian, who deduced that it therefore had a new source. Obviously it had been brought back from the moon by the crew of Apollo 11. The conjunctivitis became known as *Apollo 11* and the *Daily Times* broadcast its progress with banner headlines.

My birthday occurred two days later and my dear boss decided to help celebrate by taking eight of us, my husband, various friends, and me, out to dinner at the Chinese restaurant. He suggested I drive on our way to pick up various members of the party. His car was an Oldsmobile 98, about the same size as an entire room in my house. It had automatic transmis-sion, which was as foreign to me as the moon, and it would pass anything except a gas station. Coming towards us along two-lane Bourdillon Road was an army jeep full of yelling soldiers, traveling at great speed down the center of the road. (The usual method of progress of Nigerian army jeeps.) I kept hoping they'd get back on their side, and when I realized there was no hope of this, an emergency stop at the side of the road seemed like a good idea. The car screeched to a halt with a stench of burning rubber and one wheel listing into a storm drain. Kath was screaming, "We're on fire!"

while trying to scramble off the floor. JOS howled with laughter. He explained sweetly that when making an emergency stop with automatic transmission, one doesn't jam both feet down as is necessary with a stick shift, since one pedal is the brake but one is the accelerator. No wonder I burned rubber! Luckily the brake pedal won. I gladly reverted to my non-automatic VW Beetle.

Otherwise, it was a great birthday. It floated happily along on champagne and *toffee bananas* passed from chopstick to chopstick. Expats at the Chinese restaurant in Lagos received a lesson in civilization from the lady owner, who mandated that her food be eaten with chopsticks. If a fork was requested it would be brought, but not until the rest of the diners had almost finished their meal. In subsequent visits to southeast Asia I have frequently thanked her memory, as I have never had to go hungry through not being able to manage the utensils.

The rainy season was under way once more, so the beach was forsaken on weekends if it happened to be raining when we awoke. On days like these we would turn up at the club and sit in the bar with the week-old newspapers, and pretty soon we would be joined by others with the same amount of aimless day ahead. A few games of snooker, some darts perhaps, and then if it cleared up some might go off water skiing.

One Sunday, a war raid seemed like a good idea. Several rugby club members (who else?), armed with broom handles and anything which looked suitably weapon-like, crawled and dodged up the road to the house of Ray Sellars, another rugby club member. They climbed in through sundry windows and balconies, taking prisoners and generally demanding beer. The poor night-watch probably suffered a minor breakdown at this *t'iefman* behavior on the part of a bunch of white men. The party following the break-in was crowned by a potluck dinner for all commandos, and included the onion soup for which Ray's chef was justly famous.

Another successful Sunday enterprise was a canoe battle on Five Cowrie Creek. It occurred as a spur-of-the-moment game idea when someone offered a dash to a passing local fisherman for the use of his dugout canoe.

These flat vessels are much harder to balance in than they look, and more dashes to more fishermen resulted in a flotilla of canoes, all tipping their sunburned cargoes into the drink on an ongoing basis. The fishermen enjoyed the sight as much as those of us watching from the shade of the Flame of the Forest tree on a neighboring lawn. When anyone looked likely to actually remain upright long enough to propel the canoe in some direction, those along the shore would endeavor to sink the mariner one more time with the help of coconuts hurled from the dock. Coconut bombing turned out to be more accurate than the things they had used in the real war. There had been two "bombs" during the war while we had been living in Apapa. The Biafrans had used Molotov cocktails tossed from the open hatches of ancient DC3's to attempt to strike terror into the hearts of Lagosians. Actually, they struck righteous indignation into the hearts of expat night-clubbers, since one of the bottles made a hole in the roof above the Bagatelle. Luckily the *Baggers* was back in business in less than a week.

Coconuts made good rugby balls too, when any collection of young men was lounging around lawns waiting for curry lunches, and where the Star flowed freely.

One such day, after a curry lunch beside Five Cowrie Creek, our group surveyed the motor boats tied up to the dock and thought of a new use for one of them. Capturing the Russian flag seemed like a novel idea. Actually the only ones who were underwhelmed by this idea were the Russians. Their embassy was situated right across the river on Victoria Island. Several of us drove over in a motorboat and collected the flag. We were half way back across the creek when the presence of machine guns among the embassy guards along the shoreline persuaded us that they couldn't take a joke. We returned the flag and left.

Somehow the Russians never seemed to get into the spirit of anything. They took the Cold War rather more seriously than did the other expats along the west coast of Africa. A Russian submarine once visited Lagos. On our way back from the beach in a boat, we decided to have a look at it as we crossed the harbor. A single sentry, standing on top of the vessel and armed with a machine-gun, pointed it at us unwaveringly for the duration of the time we drove around and waved. He didn't crack a grin, either. Kath and I were particularly put out since in that woman-starved neck of the woods, the sight of two females in bikinis was always something that attracted friendly attention. We also felt that we didn't look like spies. It was certainly obvious we had no place to hide a camera.

The attitude of Greek freighter crews was much more to our liking. On another trip across the harbor the water was a bit choppy. Kath and I often took turns sitting right up on the bow of our friend Mike's small boat, where the ride was erratic and exciting. It was my turn. As we passed a Greek ship, whose entire crew appeared on deck to cheer our passing, I was knocked off by a wave. I was probably distracted. Anyway, by the time I swam back to the boat, the entire freighter had mobilized and their lifeboat was halfway launched. The sailors didn't seem at all put out at the wasted effort. Everyone called out to each other and waved happily before we resumed our expedition.

There were always a large number of boats waiting to be unloaded at Apapa, the dock area of Lagos. The official reason we understood to be something to do with the war. The real reason might have had a lot to do with *WAWA*. Some vessels were literally months waiting to be offloaded, and at one point over 120 ships were lying outside of the Lagos harbor area. It was a convenient excuse for a lack of anything at all. "It's on the way but the ship hasn't docked yet."

Unquestionably the most popular ship ever to dock at Lagos was *HMS Fearless*. This was a destroyer out of Devonport dockyard, which meant that coming from so close to Cornwall she was full of Cousin Jacks. All those displaced Cornishmen took no time at all to locate the Rugby Club and could be heard adding to the rugby song repertoire at all hours. They later told us that some sort of record had been set for the most seamen put on a charge after shore leave. Apart from the usual complement of sailors, there were 600 marines on board, so this was probably no exaggeration.

The Fearless Weekend, as it came to be known, contributed greatly to the warmth of international relations, at least between England and this particular ex-colony. We gave a rugby party for them; they invited us onto their ship and we had several parties there. All over it, in fact. They showed us the wardroom, the bar, the tanks and trucks parked below decks, another bar, the mess, a bar, etc. We all had a very good time. When we said that we hoped the *Fearless* would return, we meant it. I doubt that the Captain will ever permit it, though.

The most famous single visitor to Lagos in those days was indubitably Pele, the soccer star. Nigerians are football crazy. I swear every single one of them had to see Pele's demonstration game. I made the mistake of trying to get to Victoria Island that afternoon. The fifteen-minute drive took over three hours, due to the crowds. The soccer field was surrounded by a very high wall. It had to be high since Nigerians are very good at climbing walls. They are also unbelievably good at climbing trees. They can practically walk up trunks which appear totally smooth to the naked eye. Outside the football field the tallest trees have had pegs placed high in the trunks so that persons climbing them have some place to rest a foot while they hang twenty or thirty feet up for the time it takes to play a football match. This day there were more people than leaves in those trees. Others were doing a variety of gymnastic human-tower feats to see over the wall which would have won them instant Olympic fame.

Another visitor at this time was Harold Wilson, Britain's Labor leader. He was so unpopular with many of us who had left the U.K. that we declined attendance at the usual official receptions. We went dancing instead in a clubhouse we had made of out friend Graham's garage.

CHAPTER 22

The Ikoyi Club was more than a second home. It was really a first, since we spent more time there than at our apartment, or at the maisonette on Mekunwen Road into which we had moved after another leave. This was one of a row of pretty little one-bedroomed townhouses with circular staircases. In these dwellings, one entire wooden living-room wall rolled back to give access to the garden. I have always appreciated al fresco living. The maisonette's main advantage, however, was its proximity to the Ikoyi Club. Rarely a day passed without a visit to the club. Many days we spent four or five hours there after work, playing snooker, squash, or both. Monday and Wednesday nights were squash nights, Tuesday late afternoons were reserved for badminton. *Harry Badders*, we called it. No, I have no idea why.

There was a rule limiting the amount of time you could reserve a squash court to half an hour. This was reasonable in view of their popularity, but we felt that it wasn't worth getting *that* sweat-soaked and smelly for just a half-hour, hardy souls that we were. Only singles were played, so each partner would sign up for a consecutive half hour, and if we could find someone to brainwash into signing their name directly after ours for more time, we'd do that too. We regularly managed to stretch our games to two hours this way. The courts were indoor-outdoor, insofar as they were roofed, but a large space at the back was open to the elements. Spectators could watch from here, under the edge of the roof line, on benches reached by an outside staircase. There was no air-conditioning and no fan, so gas masks would have been appropriate attire at the end of the two hour period.

The swimming pool bar was across a narrow path from the squash courts. After our games, we could be seen crawling up the steps to the pool bar leaving a wet trail like quadrupedal slugs. Two pints of Chapman's, a glorious concoction of 7-Up, orange juice or Orange Crush, squirted with angostura bitters and anointed with citrus slices, would disappear from our glasses before we had found the strength to speak. Considering the workout our legs received every Saturday night on various nightclub dance floors, it was mildly piquing how totally a squash game in 90+ degrees could wipe us out. There was great pleasure, however, in sitting under the tropic stars and watching the subdued splashing of the lap-swimmers, feeling intoxicated by the scent of the night flowering jasmine.

While in Benin, I had been a fairly enthusiastic tennis player; particularly as there was always a ball-boy or two available for a sixpenny dash. My first squash game eliminated tennis as a hobby. The speed and excitement converted me instantly; and the squash wrist flick permanently interfered with my tennis return. Although envious of those sufficiently coordinated to play both sports well, I wasn't able to drum up the ability to fix my lapsed tennis stroke. My attitude to golf was the same. No speed and not enough excitement. Besides, I resented a sport which took at least three hours to play and three more hours to recap in the golf club bar. How can anyone remember how many hits it took, and with what, on whichever of eighteen holes? I had problems remembering the score of the squash game which I happened to be playing at the time, *and* I only had to bother with one racquet. Never mind; there were enough sports for all and almost everyone took part and enjoyed the fun in the sun.

Lagos also boasted a polo field. In some parts of Nigeria a polo pony could be obtained for as little as 25 pounds. It was deemed advisable to have four. These pieces of information came from the same person. Perhaps he was pulling my leg. He could have been, in retaliation for my disparaging remarks about his odor after a game.

There was also sailing, and the LMBC-Lagos Motor Boat Club. The sport there appeared directly related to elbow bending, either in the bar or on board any of the motor boats belonging to the members. Water-skiing was popular; and the flying club also had a fairly enthusiastic membership. The sport involved in flying included much buzzing of boats, those from the LMBC as much as the dugout canoes of the locals, who abandoned ship whenever an aircraft dived below 100 feet in their direction.

Kath's dad decided to retire. This was a large rock dropped into the pellucid waters of our contentment. Positive panic, in fact, for Kath and I. We persuaded him to let her stay with me for a final three-week vacation while the family wended their leisurely way back to U.K. via an Elder Dempster cruise. Kath agreed to fly to her new home in England when the rest of the family had moved in, but in time to help with much of the work.

I shared her consternation on the move away from the Coast. What would she do? No warmth, no stewards, no friends-yet. We commiserated: English sunshine was too thin, less than 98% humidity made our skin flake and our hair didn't look thick. What would she do with forty cocktail dresses? Who could afford to live that way in U.K? And so on, and so on.

We really lived it up that last three weeks. They went by in a blur of ball gowns still on at 5 p.m., and a lack of sleep which should have been documented for the *Guinness Book of Records*.

Too soon, she left. We sniffled. I slept. I gave up *Harry Badders*; she'd rather play than I, anyway. We wrote; long letters full of references to the technicolor of the Nigsville life and the black-and-white miseries of the U.K. winter.

Then they moved to the Canary Islands! First, Las Palmas, then to a small island off Fuerteventura named Lobos. It was warm, she felt like a real expat again, and I missed her but she was happy. I missed her dad too when he sent me a postcard addressed to *The Best Bottom in West Africa*. He said what *he* was missing was the sight of the girls walking through the club bar in their squash shorts.

At work, meanwhile, we received a nasty shock. A government missive summarily informed us, and simultaneously all other expat corporations doing business in the country, that Nigerianization would take place henceforth. This meant incorporating in Nigeria immediately; the directors to include a certain percentage of Nigerians. All expatriate jobs were to be phased out by 1975. An immediate start should be made and immigration visas would be more difficult to obtain than heretofore. And whereas, and whereas, etc. etc.

The company telex was out of order that day. Not unusual. And with probably some of the most important news ever needing transmission. *WAWA!* The document had to go in full, several legal pages. A cable would not do. The driver took me down to the GPO building, where the post and telegraph were run by one government operation as in Britain. I got an instant telex lesson from one of the operators.

"You wind dis ting, and type um heah," she told me.

It worked, more or less, and ran into several hours' telex time which could easily have been halved by an experienced operator. I imagined the furor back in the U.S. and U.K. home offices when the news hit of this latest stride in independence. Somehow, the man in the street was never sympathetic to the oil colossus when it lost millions in assets overseas due to third world edicts, riots, or Acts of God. He usually had something to say when the cost of oil rose as a result, mind.

≈≈≈

I enjoyed working and kept busy. Not all of my assigned jobs were impeccably performed. I remember one crushing failure, made all the worse owing to the Nigerianization situation and the resultant necessity of keeping our expat personnel as long as we could.

A new expat salesman wanted to be repatriated with his family, a young wife and baby. His reasons were unformulated at best. His wife and child had only been on the Coast a couple of weeks, but they *"just wanted to go home."* This state of affairs was incomprehensible to JOS and I both, and so my boss asked if I would call on Mrs. X and see if I could get to the bottom of the mystery. Anything my boss could do to make them happy, he would have done. He was a great person. Also, repatriating an entire family plus household effects less than a month after paying their way out to the Coast would of necessity dim the luster of the young man's personnel file.

Jimoh, Texaco's head driver, drove me over to the company flats. He was a tall, affable man of 17 years' accident-free experience. No small accomplishment in Lagos. He waited under a Flame tree in the compound as I climbed the stairs and knocked on the door of one of the oil company's modern, air-conditioned apartments. A young expat woman opened the door herself.

"Come on in and sit down," she said. "I've almost finished feeding the baby. Would you like a cup of coffee?" I accepted with pleasure, but when she went to make it herself I had to ask, "Where's your steward?"

"Oh, we don't have one. I like to do the work myself and we like the privacy."

I tried not to look incredulous and made small talk, working around to the $64,000 question. "I understand you aren't happy here. Is there anything at all that we could do to help the situation?"

"Oh no," she said. "We just want to go home."

I tried to point out the assets, but my Number One Gun had already been spiked-they didn't want a steward. How about the social life? The availability of sports and recreation? A nanny for the baby? I got shot down in flames so often that she could have ousted the Red Baron from his place in history. I tried another tack.

"Well, tell me what you really like to do." I felt sure I could find something to suit her.

"I like to take the baby to the park in the mornings," she answered promptly.

"You could walk to the club from here," I suggested. "There are plenty of things to do there, lots of grass (well, for a while after the rainy season!) and plenty of kids for the baby to play with."

"Oh no!" She was shocked. "It's too hot to walk!"

I pointed out as politely as I could that we were 200 miles from the equator so it was to be expected. And didn't anybody tell her that before they left England? In desperation I cast around for any straw. "There are some great jobs here too," I said. "You might be glad of that when your son goes to school."

"I'm a suburban housewife," she responded with slightly ruffled feathers. "That's what I want to be."

Were she talking in Hindustani, and the only language I spoke happened to be Gaelic, the communication gap could not have been wider. On my *wanna-be* list, suburban housewife ranked only slightly above Siberian salt-miner. I quit.

I returned to JOS with apologies for my defeat, but secure in the knowledge that England and Mrs. X deserved one another. I sincerely hoped she got rained on in the park!

The position of head of an oil company was political as well as administrative, and there were plenty of parties and receptions which JOS needed to give as well as attend. Both of our Assistant Managers had been transferred by this time. Of course their wives went with them, so we were short of official hostesses for functions. JOS himself had no wife to over-see party preparations, and the job frequently fell to me. His dear old steward, Akarta, had been with him many years. Sometimes things would get too much for him. Once he set the table for 16 for a formal dinner with the cutlery back to front. Sometimes it fell to me to run around Lagos to buy pounds of ribs, or persuade Nassar's to check out their back room for imported sauces, or see if there was a bottle of Cointreau to be found at Bhojson's Indian store.

When it is February or March and the winds gust around company headquarters in New York, Houston and London, the thought of a trip to the fleshpots on a field inspection occurs to many snowbound executives. (Their absence is, of course, always noticeable during the rainy season.) One February we hosted 12 head office visitors at one time. On this occa-sion, PanAm dropped the executives off at Lagos but gave their luggage a free ride to Hong Kong. It fell to me to track it down. The PanAm Director in Lagos was a charming man who gave me every assistance. While the airline was giving the bags another ride back from Hong Kong, however, it also fell to me to visit Leventis' department store and purchase several sets of masculine underwear in various sizes, and a dozen assorted shirts. It is usual in the tropics to change frequently, and the urge to do so is particularly strong after a seven to ten hour overnight flight.

Of course, there were plenty of catering arrangements to be made, and this while my overworked boss was having wall-to-wall meetings and mak-ing reports. Occasionally some of the executives would have a party-going expat attitude and eschew the idea of a nice dinner party on the patio of their host in favor of a nightclub-crawl hosted by the host's secretary. Oh, it was hell on the Coast, alright! Looking back on the old days of U.K. banking, I could imagine no circumstances under which they would have paid me to take half a dozen party animals dining and dancing half the night in a company-chauffeured limo. We had some serious fun!

Not only was all this stuff its own reward, but every time I did some-thing remotely outside of my job description, my charming and grateful boss would feel it necessary to reward same. Usually this was with my favorite perfume, if he were traveling through any duty-free stores. Worth's *Je Reviens* perfume was one of the hard-to-obtain items in Lagos. Otherwise he would give me chocolates, since my sweet tooth is really a whole mouthful of sweet teeth. After receipt of X number of 3 lb. ribbon-wrapped boxes of the best cocoa-butter products that Switzerland and U.K. had to offer, I was so sickened of chocolates that it became necessary to sneak down to the typing pool and hand over my latest loot to be shared among the girls.

The chocs and the nightclub visits were by no means the only perks. Since by now both Assistant Managers had been transferred, I also got the company Mercedes and its driver, Taboura.

"Well, you are doing their jobs," grinned my boss in response to my token objections.

The immigration file was also mine. It took me ten months to get approval for a new Assistant Manager, with the help of a large, serious young man named Mr. Odetoyinbo from the Personnel Department. The amount of persistence necessary to get approvals in the days of Nigerianization was unbelievable. That poor man visited the Immigration Department every business day of that ten months. By this time, my file was four inches thick. Finally persistence won out. We got a new Assistant Manager. And I got more chocolates!

CHAPTER 23

For all that such an intimidating array of shots had been necessary for access to the Coast, once there, most of us were healthier that we had been when exposed to the international influenza germs which annually scourged Europe: the Hong Kong 'flu, the Asian 'flu, and so on. *Tummy palaver*, the West African equivalent of *Montezuma's Revenge*, or *Delhi belly*, was fairly common, although that has never been a problem for me.

There was a rumor of some luckless expat walking the streets at night and being knocked into the storm drain by a Lagos bus which was turning a corner. The drains were concrete ditches deeper than the height of a man and two to five feet wide. In the dry season only a few inches of slimy water and refuse lay on the bottom. The victim's cries for help were not heard until the following morning, and exposure to whatever lived in the slimy water resulted in some terrible disease which meant his early return home, or death. The rumors never agreed on the result. Many felt it would have been understandable if he had succumbed as a result of the smell. Some of us, however, never objected to the odor of a Lagos storm drain, since it was so intermingled with the steamy heat, the streetside barbeques and food vendors, and the totally exotic nature of the place.

Food poisoning used to strike once in a while. It was hard to persuade stewards not to eat from discarded, badly dented cans. An acquaintance had thrown away a tin of peaches which gave out a minor explosion when opened, and admonished her steward not to touch it because it was bad. It looked and smelled O.K. to the steward. He fed it to his family, which proved fatal. This was an extreme case. Most times the cause of any food poisoning was not discovered and any severe stomach pains would go away in a few hours. On one occasion at work I overheard a Scot from our Operations Department saying that he needed to go home and lie down for a while.

"I think I'm having a baby," he said in his broad Highland accent; both hands clutching his midsection.

One Christmas, there was an outbreak of food poisoning which laid low almost the whole rugby club, and which we later deduced as probably being the result of the shrimp appetizer we had eaten at a large Christmas Eve party. At another party, hours later, an Australian friend's screams of agony from the bathroom ended with other club members breaking down the door and calling a doctor to administer a shot. This impressed us all. We had often enough seen our Aussie on the rugby field, and he was no sissy. He had been unable to straighten up to unbolt the door. The same cramps assailed another victim who happened to live next door to a doctor. He walked, doubled up, down his path and up the next and got his shot on the doctor's doorstep.

On Christmas Day that year, I went to the beach in the morning and spent the day surfing. An insistent stomach-ache bothered me all day, but it wasn't serious. *Iron Guts* again. Of course, I hadn't eaten many of the shrimp either, if that was in fact the culprit. It surprised me that I saw nothing of a friend who had promised to join me on the beach. On my return, I discovered that he had experienced such terrible cramps that he had fallen to the floor and had been unable to reach the phone. He was found by someone who came to launch his boat from our mutual friend's waterfront yard. More doctors and more shots. Everyone was fine next day, thank heavens.

Other inconveniences, which were part of life on the Coast, were frequently the reason for an underlying dissatisfaction which afflicted many of the expats. Minor brushes with officialdom were one instance. There was the occasion, for example, when a policeman stopped me for no obvious reason as I drove past the large roundabout-cum-fountain in Tinubu (pronounced *TIN-uhboo*) Square.

"Give me your license," he said, and popped it into his shirt pocket. "Go on!"

Idiot that I was, considering my several years' experience as a Coaster, I didn't get his number. Valid driving licenses were worth at least five pounds apiece on the black market. Numerous queries into its whereabouts yielded nothing. I got a copy and learned a lesson.

At least I didn't have to dash to get my new license; I probably would have had I been Nigerian. We did have to dash to get our new car, though. Import restrictions were imposed on almost everything during the war. Most of them could be lifted with a dash in the right direction. It cost thirty pounds to some minor official in the harbor area to obtain an import permit for a nice, new, white, shiny Volkswagen straight from the Wolfsburg factory in Germany. That same nice, new, white, shiny Volkswagen was ruined two weeks after its semi-legal entry by an uneducated local, who opened a taxi door in a narrow street just as I approached. I took the taxi door off, scared the poor passenger out of his wits, outraged the taxi driver, and dented the entire right side of my car. Then I scared the passenger some more by yelling loudly at him what I thought of him.

This kind of accident was usually resolved without the police. If the police became involved things tended to get out of hand and very expensive. They might well require a dash. Several witnesses would appear out of the woodwork. Whether or not they had witnessed anything, or even been in the same street, was of no consequence. It was a good opportunity for a dash. It seems reasonable to a poor African that if he says he saw an accident and that it was Person A's fault, then he is helping Person B who should give him a dash. Conversely, Person A might give him a bigger dash to say it was Person B's fault.

This fact-free climate engendered behavior different from that which one would exhibit in another country. One night when driving home from a nightclub, we saw a drunken soldier fall from his precarious perch on the back bumper of a Lagos bus. He fell face down on the roadway and lay there. We drove around the roundabout the opposite way and left the scene. All urges to help were squashed by the knowledge that we would have surely been accused of running him down ourselves.

Nigeria was the only country in the world where one could drive around roundabouts both ways. The traffic pattern was otherwise English, where driving should take place on the left. Many people advocated the American system of driving on the right like most of the rest of the world. With Independence, Nigerians liked to get away from some of the English systems. It was rumored that a plan had been introduced to the Lagos House of Representatives for easing the change from the left to the right side of the road. The heavy transport: mammy wagons, other trucks, and Lagos buses, would all drive on the right for a month. Meanwhile, regular traffic would still be driving on the left! Those vehicles would also change to the right side after a month. Assuming any were left?

A Shakespearean rip-off quote from my youth states that *parking is such street sorrow.* It certainly was in Lagos; and so was driving. We were wending our way slowly past the hospital at the crowded bottom end of Yakubu Gowon Street one night, when a wandering, pajama'd patient staggered into our car and fell down. He appeared to be crossing the road to another wing of the hospital. A second pajama-clad patient picked him up and they finished the journey together. Once more we left in more of a hurry than we had arrived.

Taxis tended to be a hazard too. Opening doors at whim was not the only problem the passengers posed for a taxi driver. They would frequently hop out without paying. Some wily taxi-drivers got ahead in this battle of wits by unscrewing the doorknobs to the back doors. Once the passenger had paid, the doorknobs would be retrieved from the glove compartment, screwed back in, and the imprisoned passenger was freed. This would frequently start mini-traffic jams, or compound any already in progress. Then there were the girls who hung around the major hotels smiling and waving and calling "Lift!" to any passer-by who looked to have a couple of pounds and the inclination for a quickie in the car.

There was no lack of availability of this particular physical exercise. The maitre d' at one favorite watering hole was fairly competent at acquiring attractive ladies for paying customers.

"Friday! Two to go!" did not mean that Friday should wrap up a couple of hamburgers.

CHAPTER 24

My duties as hostess eased somewhat when my boss met up with an old friend from previous days when they had been posted simultaneously to the Congo. A very tall and elegant Dutch girl, she had become the new secretary to the head of Shell Oil Company. Her name was Lukina. Her English was perfect, and in fact she was fluent in six languages. She was also some cook.

I noticed a new spring in my boss's ever-cheerful stride. You had to look carefully; he was never a complainer on the worst of days.

The practical joking between JOS and his English friend Reggie became more frenetic. Reggie was manager of the Congo branch of Texaco at the time. Many of the cables coming in from Brazzaville and marked *Confidential* would have me tearing out lumps of hair when my code book would not reveal contents of any sense. Reggie thought it was fun to confuse his old friend with this rubbish. I had a rather jaundiced view of the whole thing because I was the one confused; but enjoyed my revenge when JOS let me write rubbish back. I wonder if Reggie's secretary had to deal with it?

An infection with which the Lagos hospital system was totally unable to deal sent Lukina home to Holland on a stretcher, complete with IV's and a charter flight. My boss was uncharacteristically terse and unsmiling, and started to grab his private line before I got *"Mr. Sheldon's Office"* out of my mouth. We received good news in a couple of days and things started to relax. As Lukina recovered, the rubbish cables started up again and I got chocolates. All was well.

Things heated up at work as the east opened up. Eventually, self-proclaimed Premier Ojukwu was defeated and the Federal troops regained possession of the remaining rebel-held territory. Squads of expats went down to the eastern states to check out what was left of their companies' property, and in some cases their own. Many easterners who had been lost to us in their home states came back to work.

Texaco had its share of returning personnel, and there were reams of reports to be typed, telexed and cabled. There was much reconstruction to do and inventories to be made and restocked. We worked harder and later. I ate more chocolates. The diversion was welcome. My domestic life was not running as smoothly as everything else. My husband and I had successively worse rows and were becoming more and more estranged. He went out with the boys. I went out with the boys. On one occasion we met in the club after two and a half days.

"Oh, are you still here?" he cracked.

Things weren't always so cordial, however.

"I can do anything I want. You won't leave me. You love Nigeria too much!"

He was hitting below the belt there. And I gave as good as I got. One night in the bedroom I was losing an argument. Never marry someone with a great sense of humor if you want to win arguments. The other side of that coin is an ability to flay you with his tongue. Things escalated to the point of flying hairbrushes, and then came knocking on the wall from the adjacent maisonette. So, the next day while my husband was at work, I moved out. My boss, whose shoulder got thoroughly soggy during the recounting of my side of the story, gave me the use of one of the Assistant Manager's houses with its three stewards and three fridges. Sunday and my driver helped me move my clothes, my Elvis record collection, and a steamed pudding pot which I figured would be hard to replace. I didn't want to be bothered with anything else. I had a good job and felt I had enough ability to keep myself.

Later, I got a telephone call from Tom. "I see you moved out," he said.

"Yeh."

"I figured you meant it when I saw that your Elvis collection was gone."

So that was that. The end of eleven years together. I felt such a failure. There would be a divorce, of course. No one in my family had ever been divorced before. In fact, in those days in England I hardly knew anyone who had been divorced. If they were, the reasons were dissected, clucked over, and the worst assumed. I cried. I would lose my beloved in-laws. I cried some more. Poor JOS lived with a perennially soaking shoulder.

On the other hand, my new home was wonderful. It had a small flagged patio under a frangipani tree which proved perfect as a breakfast location, and I invited a series of friends over on the days before we went to the beach. We drank Mateus rose (which was very popular in the late '60's; I cannot think why) and hung the empty wine bottles from the bare branches of the frangipani like some esoteric Christmas ornaments. I was never in for lunch or dinner. The social life was even more dizzying for a single woman.

Then the worst possible blow fell. My work permit would not be renewable owing to being a *Form B: Accompanying Husband*. A *Form A* was necessary to reside alone and I didn't have about ten months to get one, assuming persistence might possibly pay off in this instance. My boss spoke to everyone he could; so did I. Returning to a failed marriage was out of the question. Once that kind of decision is made, for me it's irrevocable.

I was unbelievably miserable. Where would I go? I didn't *want* to go! How could I live without my beloved Nigsville? I *refused* to go back to U.K! What would I do? Panic. Panic. I cried some more.

Salt was rubbed into the fresh wound. I had a beautiful friend named Jane, also a west country girl. She had long, blonde hair and green eyes, worked for the High Commission as a secretary, and was a great cook. There she was, practically a goddess, and living in a paradise of single men. Her long-standing love affair with a good-looking rake named Tony, of whom I never did approve, was over. Her tour wasn't over. She cried. I cried because I didn't want to go home and I had to. She cried because she did want to go home and couldn't. It was funny in a masochistic sort of way.

I made the most of the social round to network, but Nigerianization had put severe limitations on personnel. My parents wrote to say that I could have their savings for a ticket home. I was touched. We never had any money when I was growing up, and now when they had got rid of their offspring and had finally been able to save a few pounds they were ready to give it to me. However, no way would I run home to momma even if I wanted to!

For a long time Lebanon had been high on my mental list of places to visit. The Middle East Airlines brochures floating about Lagos promised the treasures and pleasures of the Mediterranean with technicolor photos of Baalbeck, the Bay of Junieh, the Hotel Phoenicia, the Corniche, the beaches, the restaurants, the nightclubs…. I decided that I would go to Beirut. I would find a job, perfect my Arabic, eat *mezze* every day, and plot incessantly to get back to the Coast.

Jane gave a goodbye party for me. The radio played *I'm Leaving on a Jet Plane.* We both burst into tears again.

Our Lebanese friend Shakey from *Antoine's* was going back to Beirut for a few weeks' leave. He was chaperoning the daughter of some family friends. Her name was Houda. I knew her from several meetings at the restaurant. We arranged to take the same flight. Shakey promised he would introduce me to all sorts of people in Beirut who would be bound to help with my plans.

I went over to the bank to say goodbye to my spouse. He told me that he had sacked Sunday.

"What on earth for?" I asked, not envying him the task of finding another steward as good at curry. Tom explained that he had bought a new car, a large, comfortable Peugeot. It had suffered a flat tire one night half a mile down the road. It was late so he left it and walked home. Sunday, who still fancied himself as a driver, decided to drive the car, still on the wheel rim, back to the house. Of course the wheel rim was ruined, but so was one entire side of the car since Sunday misjudged the entrance to the carport. We didn't have much luck with the sides of our cars. We commiserated over our various troubles, and said we'd see one another at the divorce.

"Hey, mate!" he called out as I turned to leave. "You've still got great legs!" I had to grin. Sometimes it was possible to remember why I had married him in the first place.

CHAPTER 25

Doomsday arrived. Like most other Lagos days, it was cloaked in sunshine. The palm trees waved and the sea sparkled.

At the airport, the porter and the driver handed over my seven suitcases for weighing. The airline clerk asked for seventy-two pounds and change for my excess baggage charges. Then he slid off his stool, leaned around a corner and beckoned conspiratorially.

"Gimme two pound," he said with a wink. My last dash! I thought with sorrow. There really were advantages to the system and I was going to miss it.

We walked across the tarmac to the waiting plane. I had worn my leopard-print refugee dress in the forlorn hope that it might bring me the same kind of luck as when my last reluctant leave-taking had landed me in Lagos.

No thunderbolt from God atomized the plane. No *Form-A* waving deliverer, black or white, ran towards me across the tarmac. A spattering of late season raindrops hissed onto the engines of the Boeing 727. Tears misted my last sight of the glorified shacks which comprised the airport buildings, and the tall, slender palms on the low horizon.

It would be hell, no longer being on the Coast.

THE END

ABOUT THE AUTHOR

Some thirty-five years after the events in this book, Chris Meier resides in Florida with her American husband, Pete, and their two grown daughters, Lisa and Lori. She wrote the book in response to requests from some Old Coasters who also still miss the good old days, and agreed to publish it in response to requests from her daughters.

GLOSSARY

Nigerian/Other	English
Ahwe	(Arabic) Coffee
Ahwe-min-hel	(Arabic) Coffee with cardamom seed flavoring
Alhaji	Moslem who has made a pilgrimage to Mecca
Anti-t'ief	Anti thief
Artra	Bleaching cream used to lighten skin
Apollo 11	Conjunctivitis
Binni	Tribe from Benin
BOAC	British Overseas Airways Corporation
Bush	(n.) Location with few people.
	(adj.) Uneducated, lacking in amenities.
Calabash	Gourd
Chop	(n.) Food.
	(v.) To eat. To kill.
Coaster	Person living in West Africa
Cousin Jack	Cornishman
Coy-o	Binni greeting
Dash	Gift, bribe
Duck-billed women	Tribal members with calabash plugs in lips and earlobes
Eid-el-Fitri	Moslem religious holiday
ECN	Electricity Company of Nigeria
Emir	Northern tribal chief
Expatriate, expat	Person living in a foreign country
Fattouche	Lebanese salad with lemon dressing & toasted pita bread

Gari	Cassava, Nigerian staple food
Gecko	Small, colorless house lizard, which eats mosquitoes
Hausa	Northern Nigerian tribe. (Predominantly Moslem)
Harmattan	Period in Dec-Jan when Sahara dust travels many miles
High life	Popular Nigerian dance music
House of Joy	Brothel
Hummus	Lebanese chickpea dip
Ibo	Tribe from SE region of Nigeria. (Predominantly Christian)
Juju	Voodoo
Jungle juice	Fresh fruit salad
Kafta	Finger-shaped grilled Lebanese spiced ground meat
Knicker-for-up	(Nigerian) Brassiere
Knickers	(English) Panties
Korna	(Northern Nigeria) Corner
Laterite	Red road material: dust in dry season, mud in rains
Mallam	Mister (Moslem title)
Madame	Lady of the house
Master	Head of household employing local stewards, drivers, etc.
Mau-mau	Tribe from East Africa
Mezze	Selection of Arabic appetizers
Migardi	Night watchman (see also *nightwatch*)
NIFOR	Nigerian Institute For Oil-Palm Research, in Mid-West
Nightwatch	Night watchman (see also *Migardi*)
Palaver	Talk, argument, problem, strife
Pickin	Child
PCV	Peace Corps Volunteer (American)
Ramon	(Arabic) Pomegranate
Ramadan	Moslem holy period
Rank-a-diddy	Hausa greeting
Sabon-Gari	Foreigners' quarter in Kano. Tribes from other regions lived here.
Salah	(Arabic) Prayer, Moslem holiday.

Sanu	Hausa greeting
Savvy book	Be able to read
S'bagh el khaire	(Arabic) Good morning
Small	A little bit, a little while
Small small	A very little bit, a very little while
Small boy	Steward's helper
Snooker	Game rather like the American *pool*, played on a billiard table
Steward	House boy, major-domo
Stinkfish	Foul-smelling powdered dried fish used as condiment
T'iefman	Thief
The Troubles	Inter-tribal warfare (particularly used of pre-civil war strife)
Tummy palaver	Diarrhea, (Nigerian *Montezuma's Revenge*)
VSO	Voluntary Service Overseas volunteer (British)
WAWA!	West Africa Wins Again! (Used after inefficiencies)
White Man's Grave	West Coast of Africa
Worrdi	(Arabic) Rose
Yoruba	Tribe from Western area of Nigeria
Zaranda	Village where *duck-billed* women live
Zukeipa	(Northern Nigeria) Zoo keeper

Made in the USA
Monee, IL
21 March 2021